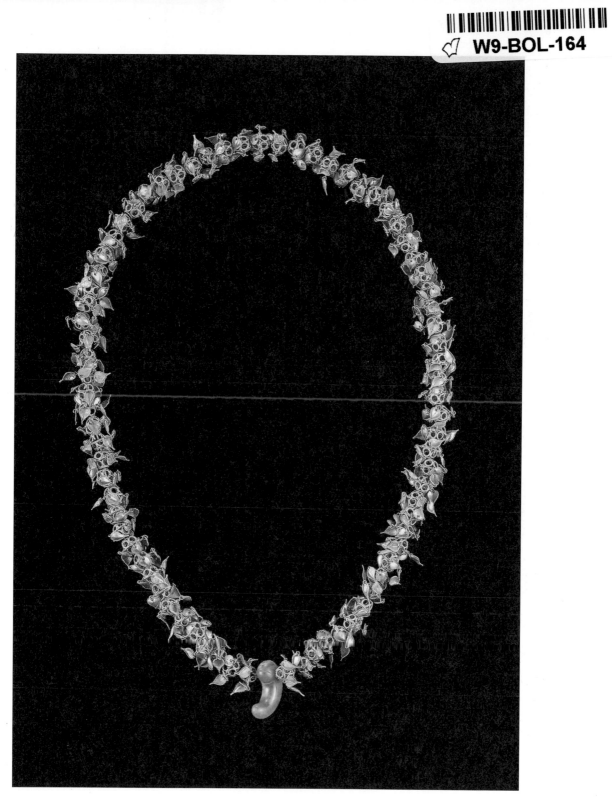

Gold Necklace

6th century AD, Silla Dynasty, Length 30.3cm, Seoul National Museum

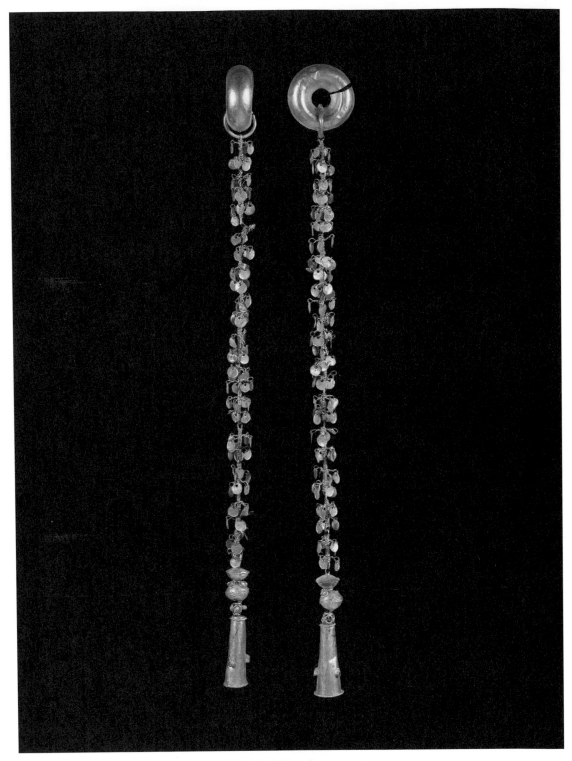

Gold Pendants

4th century AD, Silla Dynasty, Length 26.4cm, Kyongju National Museum

Gold Pendants

5th century AD, Silla Dynasty, Length16.8cm, Kyongju National Museum

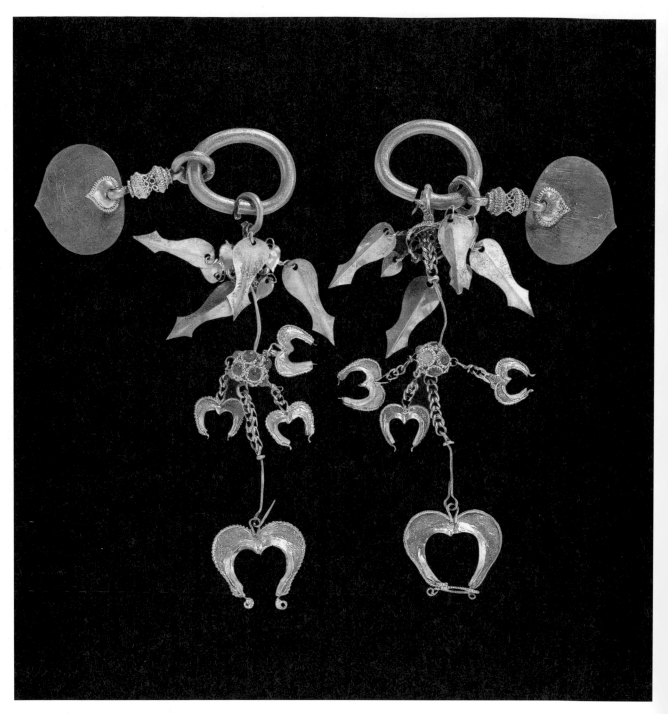

Gold Earrings

5th century AD, Silla Dynasty, Length 9.7cm, Kyongju National Museum

The heart-shaped decorative attachments were designed to hold jewels such as red or green jade. The earrings were attached directly to a crown or hat with strings or thread, so as to hang next to the ears.

Fifty Wonders of Korea

Volume 1. Culture and Art

Edited and Published by

Korean Spirit & Culture Promotion Project

Fifty Wonders of Korea

Volume 1. Culture and Art

Edited and Published by

Korean Spirit & Culture Promotion Project

http://www.kscpp.net

Printed and Bound by

Samjung Munhwasa

Chungjeong-ro 37-18, Seodaemun-gu, Seoul

ISBN: 978-0-9797263-1-6

First print, December 2007

Second print, October 2008

Printed in the Republic of Korea

Contents

Contributors of Images

We would like to express our gratitude to the following organizations and individuals for their kind permission to reproduce images in this book.

Garam Publishing Company
Hyundae Bulkyo
National Museum of Korea, Seoul
National Museum of Korea, Kimhae
National Museum of Korea, Kyongju
Samsung Museum of Art, Leeum
Silla Arts and Science Museum
Sol Publishing Company
Kang So-yon (Professor of Hongik University)
Kang Woo-bang (Director of Illhyang Institute of Korean Art History)

Note on Romanization

The Romanization of Korean words in this book follows the McCune-Reischauer system, except in the case of prominent cultural assets, figures and place names for which alternative usages are better known, and of individuals who have expressed a preference for alternative spellings of their names.

Preface

Among the nations of East Asia, Korea is one of those lesser known to the West. However, as you learn more about the country, you will find that it contains many wonders. After the tragedy of the Korean War in 1950, Korea was divided and left in great poverty. Over the past few decades, South Korea has been dramatically transformed from one of the world's poorest countries to the 10th to 12th largest economy in the world, and is now home to household names such as Samsung, LG and Hyundai. At the start of the 21st century, Korean popular culture, in particular its music, movies and TV shows, has gained huge popularity not only in Asia but also the rest of the world, a phenomenon known as the *Hallyu* or the "Korean wave." However, Korea's rich and unique cultural heritage, accumulated over the course of its long history, still remains largely unknown and undiscovered.

In this book, *Fifty Wonders of Korea*, we have selected fifty achievements of Korea's past, dating from ancient to pre modern times, which can be regarded as among the world's greatest cultural and scientific legacies. They are discussed in two volumes, under the themes of *Culture and Art* and *Science and Technology*.

Part One of the first volume, Printing, Language & History, begins with an account of the moveable metal type, which was invented in Korea some 200 years before the days of Gutenberg. It also includes a discussion of the Korean alphabet, considered to be the world's most scientific and rational writing system, and other items that are designated as national treasures or registered in the UNESCO "Memory of the World" program.

Part Two, Fine Art, begins with the spectacular gold crowns of ancient Silla, and also discusses ten other works of Korean art acclaimed not only as masterpieces in their own country but also the world. In 1922, when Korea was under colonial rule and knowledge of its history and art was suppressed, the Japanese scholar Yanagi Muneyoshi said, "If a righteous historian were to write a book on the history of Korean art, it would surely amaze the people of the world." Perhaps with these words in mind, the German scholar Andre Eckardt wrote *A History of Korean Art* in the late 1920s. He was the first western scholar to write on this subject, and stated in his book, "It can be reasonably asserted that Korea has produced the most beautiful or, put more strongly, the most consummate and accomplished works of art in East Asia."

In the second volume, we will explore the history of science and technology in Korea, which, as it will be seen, is more astonishing than the rapid economic growth of the country in recent times. We will examine thirty achievements and discoveries made in the field of scientific invention and research, including the astronomical inscriptions recently discovered on dolmen stones from the 30th century BC, erected 1800 years before the boundary stones of Mesopotamia, which were previously believed to be the earliest examples of astronomical observations inscribed on ancient stones.

We hope that readers will learn much about Korean and East Asian civilization through the discussions of these fifty wonders. We are deeply grateful to the many scholars, museums, and other organizations who contributed to this publication with advice and insights, and also for their kind permission to reproduce the pictures in this book.

Map of Korea and neighboring countries

Timeline of Korean History

BC 700,000~BC 8000	Paleolithic Period
BC 8000~BC 2000	Neolithic Period
BC 2333~BC 108	Old Choson Dynasty: The First Kingdom of Korea (Bronze Age & Iron Age)
BC 57~AD 668	Three Kingdoms Period: Koguryo, Paekche and Silla
AD 668~AD 935	Unified Silla
AD 918~AD 1392	Koryo Dynasty
AD 1392~AD 1910	Choson Dynasty
AD 1910~AD 1945	Japanese Occupation
AD 1945	Korea divided into North and South
AD 1950~1953	Korean War

Source: National Institute of Korean History (2007)

Human life in the Korean peninsula can be traced back to the Paleolithic era of 700,000 years ago. The roots of Korean culture started to form around BC 8000. Examples of so-called "comb-pattern" pottery, which began to appear in the peninsula around BC 5000, are among the most well-known and important archeological relics of the Neolithic Age. The first kingdom of Korea was called *Choson* ("Land of Morning Calm"). It was founded by Tangun Wanggum in BC 2333, on the principle of *Hongik Ingan*, which means "to live and act for the benefit of all mankind." The two volumes of *Fifty Wonders of Korea* discuss legacies from this Old Choson dynasty (BC 2333~BC 108) through to the later Choson dynasty (AD 1392~AD 1910). All of them are direct and vivid sources of Korea's past, and reflect the diverse colors of Korean culture. It is hoped that the reader, after enjoying this book, will continue to explore further and gain a deeper understanding of what has nourished the spirit of Korea over the centuries.

Part One

Printing, Language & History

1. Invention of Moveable Metal Type

In a recent list by *Time* magazine of the greatest inventions made in the past thousand years, the first place was awarded to the invention of moveable metal type. The 1995 year-end edition of the *Washington Post*, and also a special edition of *Life* magazine in 1997, both selected moveable metal type as the most significant discovery to be made in the history of the world. The reason that moveable metal type is valued so highly is because it played a critical role in the development of human civilization.

Before printing was invented, each letter of a book had to be copied out by hand using a pen or brush. Book production required a great amount of time and effort, and each volume was extremely expensive. As a result, it was difficult for literary works to be distributed very far or quickly. However, with the invention of moveable type, several pages could be printed in short succession, rather than having to write them out letter by letter. In other words, mass production of books became possible, and through the swift diffusion of information that followed, science and literature took great steps forward, and civilization could make faster progress.

A remarkable fact, little known in the West, is that the method of printing using moveable metal type, which contributed so much to mankind's development, was first used in Korea 200 years before the first European printing press was made by Gutenberg in 1455.

In 1234, when the Mongols invaded Korea, the Koryo dynasty (918~1392) moved its capital to Kanghwa Island in order to launch a defense campaign. A record from this time has survived to tell us that a collection of Zen Buddhist writings by the Monk Hyon-gak, originally printed using metal type, was reprinted using woodblock in 1239. A renowned scholarly official Yi Kyubo relates that *Prescribed Ritual Texts of the Past and Present* (*Sangjong Kogum Yemun*) was republished in 1234 using metal type, as its pages had become worn and its letters were fading. These historic records show that metal type was being used in Korea during the Koryo dynasty before the year 1234.

The origins of the moveable metal print in Korea are becoming acknowledged by the rest of the world. In the Japanese *World Encyclopedia*, it is stated, "Near the close of the 12th century, printing with moveable metal type began in Korea. This was the world's first metal type printing." The English author John Man, a leading writer on Gutenberg, also confirms in his books *The Gutenberg Revolution* and *Alpha Beta* that the fifty-volume *Prescribed Ritual Texts of the Past and Present* published during the Koryo dynasty in 1234 is the world's first example of moveable metal type printing.

It is not by chance that Koreans came to be the first to use metal type print. The country had enjoyed a strong literary tradition from ancient times, and by the 12th century books were in great demand and faster and more efficient methods were required to produce them.

In 1123, a Song Chinese civil officer, Xu Jing, accompanied an official embassy to Korea, and recorded his impressions of the country in a journal. In this journal, published as *Illustrated Record of the Chinese Embassy to Koryo During the Xuanhe Era* (*Xuanhe fengshi Gaoli tujing*), he described the zeal for education in early 12th century Korea:

> In every street and village, you will find both public and private schools, where the children of commoners and those unmarried

learn literature from a teacher. When they come of age, they go to study in Buddhist temples with other students. Even children of a very young age are taught by village teachers. It is a truly commendable state of affairs. The people of Koryo consider it shameful not to be well-versed in literature.

Though Korea was at the time a hierarchical society, in which the nobility and the commons were kept apart, ready access to information and knowledge had long been the established norm. As a result, school education was available even to children in the lower ranks of society. Korea's devotion to education and the study of literature would later impress many other foreigners. A British scholar reflected, *"When our ancestors had one Chaucer, Koryo had many great writers, and all the people of Koryo revered books."* Joubert, an officer in the French naval force which invaded Kanghwa Island in 1866, wrote in an account of his travels in *Le Tour du Monde* magazine (1873), "The fact that books can be found even in the house of a poor peasant is something that we can only look upon with admiration and humbled pride."

The invention of moveable metal type was a natural development for a country dedicated to learning and literature, and the new metal type contributed greatly to the growth of culture in East Asia.

Regrettably, few of the earlier metal type prints have survived. The second volume of *Buljo Jikji Simche Yojeol* (generally known as *Jikji* for short, printed in 1377 and predating Gutenberg's printing press by 78 years) is currently housed in the National Library of France, testifying that Korea was the original inventor of moveable metal type.

Jikji was published by Sokchan and Taljam, disciples of the Grand Master Paekwun Hwasang, who wished to spread their Master's teachings, and it was printed by the Hungdok Temple of Chungju Province in July 1377, three years after the Grand Master had passed away. At the beginning of 20th century, it was added to the collection of Collin de Plancy, who was serving as French consul in Seoul. At an auction in 1911, the book passed into the hands of the collector Henri Véver, and when he died in 1950, it was donated to the National Library of France, where it has been kept ever since.

Forgotten for some years after, *Jikji* was re-discovered by Dr. Park Byeng-Sen, a Korean assistant at the National Library of France. It would go on to receive worldwide attention when it was displayed in the 1972 "Le Livre" exhibition held by UNESCO. The French media of the day were greatly impressed, with newspaper headlines and television programs reporting the news that moveable metal type printing had existed in Korea before it emerged in Europe.

In 2001, *Jikji* was inscribed in UNESCO's "Memory of the World" register. The decision was explained as follows:

> *Buljo Jikji Simche Yojeol* is the world's oldest extant metal type print, and had a profound impact on the spread of the printing culture and human history. We therefore recognize it as a documentary heritage of global significance, and also took into account its rarity as the only book of its kind existing in the world. *Jikji* and the Gutenberg Bible are the two oldest metal type prints to have been produced in the East and the West, and constitute a great heritage that changed the documentation culture of the human race. Based on the spirit of The Memory of the World Programme, UNESCO hereby recommends its inclusion in the Register.

In 2004, UNESCO's Executive Board approved the establishment of a "Jikji Memory of the World Prize," consisting of an award of US$ 30,000 to be given every two years to individuals or institutions who make significant contributions to the preservation and accessibility of documentary heritage.[1]

As UNESCO recognizes, *Jikji* lives on not only as part of Korea's heritage, but also as one of the great cultural legacies of the world.

---

[1] Source: http://portal.unesco.org/

2. Invention of Lead-Based Type

By the time Gutenberg had begun using moveable metal type in the 15th century, type-printing of this kind was no longer uncommon in Korea. The era of Gutenberg (1397~1468) and his achievements in Germany corresponds with the life and reign of King Sejong the Great (1397~1450) in Korea. During the king's 32-year reign, a large number of books were printed with moveable type, covering a wide range of subjects, including Confucianism, Buddhism, Literature, Education, Law, Agriculture, Medicine, History, Music, Mathematics, and Astronomy.

Under King Sejong, the design of the typeface was also improved, in order to make the appearance of the text more defined and regular. The *Kabin* font, cast in 1434, became the most popular type of the Choson period (1392~1910), and was re-cast more than seven times before the 20th century.

A noteworthy feature of this beautiful type was the alloy technique used to make it. According to Professor Sohn Pow-key of Yonsei University, the strength of the brass used in the casting of the *Kabin* font is comparable in strength to the metal used in present day U.S. Navy artillery. Spectrographic analysis shows that it consisted of 84% copper, 3~7% zinc, 5% lead, and 0.1% iron, and was thus the ideal alloy for casting type.

After many attempts, Korea eventually succeeded in producing the world's first lead-based type. King Sejong and his scientists could not have achieved this without an accurate understanding of the properties of lead. Lead has a lower melting point than other metals, and also cools quickly, which is an advantage when making large-type letters. Since the academic world regards lead-based type as the father of modern type, Korea can be regarded not only as the origin of moveable metal type, but also a pioneer in modern type as well.

The lead-based Pyongjin type (1436) was created because King Sejong wanted to provide larger typefaces for the elderly and those with failing eyesight. One of the books printed using this type was the historical work, *Chachi Tonggam Kangmok*. The work consisted of 294 volumes, each 76 pages in length. King Sejong ordered around 600 copies of this book to be published. At a total of over 12 million pages, this was a truly astonishing achievement.

3. The World's Oldest Woodblock Print

Traditionally, there have been two main printing techniques in Asia, those of woodblock printing and moveable type printing. In the woodblock technique, ink is applied to letters carved upon a wooden board, which is then pressed onto paper. With moveable type, the board is assembled using different letter-types, according to the page being printed. Wooden printing was used in the East from the 8th century onwards, and moveable metal type came into use during the 12th century.

Korea is not only the inventor of moveable metal type, but is also home to the earliest example of woodblock printing. In October 1966, *The Great Dharani Sutra of Undefiled Pure Radiance* (often referred to simply as the *Dharani Sutra*), was discovered within the Shakyamuni Pagoda of Pulguksa Temple in Kyongju. Printed using twelve wooden boards, the scroll measures 8cm in width and 6.2m in length. Since it is believed that the Shakyamuni Pagoda was completed in AD 751, the print is therefore at least as old as the shrine in which it was stored.

Before the discovery of the *Dharani Sutra*, the world's oldest woodblock print was a copy of the *Diamond Sutra*, discovered by the British archaeologist Marc Aurel Stein at Dunhuang in China. This sutra was printed in AD 868, and so the *Dharani Sutra* discovered in Korea predates it by at least 117 years.

The discovery of the *Dharani Sutra* caused much controversy amongst academics. Many found it difficult to believe that a woodblock print, which

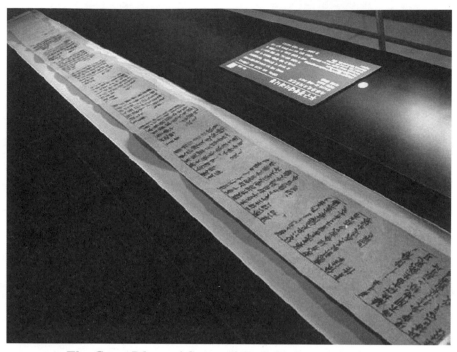

The Great Dharani Sutra of Undefiled Pure Radiance
Early 8th century AD, National Treasure No. 126, Seoul National Museum

appeared to have been made earlier than the oldest surviving example in China, could have been produced in Korea and not within China itself. Up to this point, it had been assumed that China was the inventor of woodblock printing. However, efforts to ascertain the exact time and circumstances of the printing of the sutra continued, and in the end, various critical pieces of evidence confirmed that the *Dharani Sutra* had indeed been printed in Korea, and even earlier than AD 751.

The *Dharani Sutra* features eight instances of four words that were in official use only during the years AD 690~704, and in complete disuse by AD 722. Furthermore, an inscription on the outer container of a *sarira* reliquary made in AD 706, discovered in a nearby temple site in Kyongju, states that the

18

Dharani Sutra was enshrined at the same time as the reliquary. Expert analysis comparing this inscription with the letters of the *Dharani Sutra* revealed that they had been written by the same person. These investigations established that the *Dharani Sutra* was printed in 706, when the *sarira* reliquary was enshrined within the Three-Storey Pagoda at the Hwangboksa Temple.[2]

The *Dharani Sutra* scroll is currently being kept at the Seoul National Museum. In a published study, a Japanese printing researcher remarked:

> The letters are exceptionally beautiful in form. The writing of the *Dharani Sutra* text discovered at Million Pagoda is quite crude, but this text is written in a dignified script which has reached a greater level of refinement. I believe that by the time this *Dharani Sutra* was printed, the country's woodblock technique was already at a considerably advanced stage. The thin paper, measuring 8cm in width, appears to be *Hanji* [traditional handmade Korean paper]. Even though the paper has been discolored, the ink is still very clear and distinct.

Already in the early 8th century, Korea's printing techniques had made considerable progress. In his famous book *The Discoverers*, the prominent American historian and critic Daniel J. Boorstin singled out Korea as the "most developed nation in the field of printing." In the next chapter, we will examine the *Tripitaka Koreana*, one of the most important milestones in the history of printing in Korea.

---

[2] The dating of the *Dharani Sutra* is discussed in detail in Dr. Kim Sung-soo's *Study of the Great Dharani Sutra of Undefiled Pure Radiance*, published by the Cheongju Early Printing Museum in 2002.

4. The Tripitaka Koreana

In Haeinsa Temple, a thousand-year-old monastery located in the southeastern part of Korea, the *Tripitaka Koreana* is kept and preserved to this day. The *Tripitaka Koreana* is a national treasure of Korea and registered as part of UNESCO's "Memory of the World" programme.

Tripitaka is a Sanskrit word meaning "three baskets," and refers to the teachings of the Buddha (*Sutra Pitaka*), the precepts followed by monks and lay followers (*Vinaya Pitaka*), and commentaries on these two scriptures (*Abhidharma Pitaka*). The word *Tripitaka* is used to refer to these three scriptures together.

In order to preserve the teachings of the Shakyamuni Buddha for eternity, 20 different versions of the *Tripitaka* were made in Asia. The *Tripitaka Koreana* is considered the most comprehensive and accurate of them all. Moreover, while the woodblocks used to print the other *Tripitaka* collections have almost all been lost, and only the printed scripts remain, the woodblocks of the *Tripitaka Koreana* have survived in perfect condition.

A Remarkable Feat in the History of Printing

The *Tripitaka Koreana*, completed in 1251, was made using a total of 81,258 woodblocks that altogether weighed about 280 tons. Each block is roughly 4 centimeters thick. If they were piled up, they would reach a height of 3,200 meters, higher than Mount Paekdu (2,744m), the tallest mountain in the Korean peninsula. There are 52,382,960 characters engraved on the woodblocks. If one read the *Tripitaka* at a rate of four to five thousand characters a day, it would take 30 years to complete.

The *Tripitaka Koreana* could be considered the finest of the *Tripitaka* collections that were produced in East Asia, not only in terms of its size, but also its thoroughness and accuracy, and the beauty of its engraved characters.

Because it draws on the previous *Tripitakas* produced by other nations, the content of *Tripitaka Koreana* is very rich. It can therefore be used to study the Northern Song Chinese *Tripitaka*, of which little has survived for example. The *Tripitaka Koreana* also contains scriptures that were not included in the *Tripitakas* published either before or after it was made.

Because the *Tripitaka Koreana* was so comprehensive and rich in content, it became a model for the Japanese *Tripitaka Sinsu*, the Chinese *Tripitaka Pingajungsa*, and the Taiwanese *Tripitaka Pulgwang*. In this current age, when many Sanskrit classical texts have been lost altogether, the *Tripitaka Koreana* is not only an important repository of Buddhist philosophy, but also an important tool in understanding the history of Buddhism in Korea, China, and other East Asian countries.

The *Tripitaka Koreana* is also remarkably accurate. This is due to the efforts of the Venerable Sugi, an abbot of Kaetaesa temple and a renowned scholar monk, who had compared every version of the *Tripitaka* in existence at the time, and made corrections where a character was missing or erroneous. Accordingly, the *Tripitaka Koreana* is recognized by the Buddhist scholars of the world as the most accurate of its kind.

Although made in the 13th century, the beauty of the characters engraved upon the woodblocks far exceeds that of later *Tripitakas* produced in the 17th

A Woodblock of *Tripitaka Koreana*

and 18th centuries. The task of inscribing the letters was accomplished by a team of around thirty engravers. Even though many people were involved, the characters are consistent in form as if one skillful engraver had carved them all, and each character is pleasing to look at.

How the *Tripitaka Koreana* was made

The making of the *Tripitaka Koreana*, which took 16 years, began when the Mongols invaded Koryo Korea (AD 918~1392) in the mid-13th century. It was made in the belief that the power of Buddha would ward off the forces of the enemy.

To make the woodblocks, they chose trees that were at least 50 or 60 years old, and cut them into logs during wintertime. Logs that are cut during winter are denser and do not easily become warped. In order to help the wood retain its shape and to prevent decay, the logs then underwent a long and complex treatment process.

First, they were kept in sea water for three years to remove every trace of resin. They were then cut into equal lengths and boiled in salt water. The salt water prevented insect infestations and mold, and also distributed moisture evenly throughout the wood. They were then dried in a well-ventilated enclosure for another three years. Once they were completely dry, the woodblocks were sanded and their surfaces made smooth.

After this lengthy process, the engravers began to inscribe the *Tripitaka* scriptures on the surface of the wood. This was performed with great devotion, and it is said that they bowed down to Buddha before engraving each letter. Because of such devotion, there are almost no mistaken or missing letters in the *Tripitaka Koreana*. Such a feat is rare in the history of woodblock printing, and can almost be regarded as a miracle.

Once the engraving was complete, lacquer was applied to the woodblocks. Lacquer not only repels insects, but is also highly resistant to water and chemicals. Since it adheres strongly to the wood, it served an important function in protecting the Tripitaka woodblocks.

Finally, rectangular wooden bars were added to both sides of the woodblocks to prevent warping, and the four corners were decorated with copper fittings. Academics were surprised to discover that the copper used to decorate the woodblocks was 99.6% pure. Technology capable of refining metals to such a degree must have been rare in the 13th century. Even the nails, which were used to attach these copper fittings, were pure to between 94.5% and 96.8%. Made with low-carbon steel, they included 0.33%-0.38% manganese, and hardly any of them have rusted.

As it can be seen, the making of the *Tripitaka Koreana* was an achievement made possible by great effort, as well as the earnest prayers of monks, scholars, technicians, and many others. In their attempts to ward off a foreign invasion, Koreans gave their all to the project, making use of the most advanced technology and expertise available at the time. As a result, the 81,258 woodblocks of the *Tripitaka Koreana* have retained their original condition to this day, over seven hundred fifty years after they were made.

Continuing in the spirit of their ancestors, Koreans are still contributing to the *Tripitaka Koreana* project. In 2000, after nine years of work involving one hundred experts and a cost of eight million dollars, the digitalization of the *Tripitaka Koreana* was completed. A project was also begun in 2004 to transfer the *Tripitaka Koreana* inscriptions on to copperplate. Since woodblocks have a lifespan of about 1000 years, whereas copperplate has a lifespan of 10,000 years, this is an important undertaking if the *Tripitaka Koreana* is to be preserved in its physical form.

The Secret of 750 Year Preservation

The depository buildings which house the *Tripitaka Koreana* are unique. Officially the largest wooden storage complex in the world, they are registered together with the *Tripitaka* as part of the UNESCO World Heritage.

At first, the *Tripitaka Koreana* woodblocks were stored at Kanghwa Island. Since 1398, they have been kept in Haeinsa temple. Haeinsa temple was considered an ideal place to store the *Tripitaka Koreana*. It is located in the south of Korea, beyond the reach of enemy forces invading from the north, and is also far inland, safe from invasions by pirates.

The depository buildings at Haeinsa temple have 108 columns, which symbolize the 108 defilements. By placing the words of Buddha within a house of defilements, it shows that enlightenment exists within these defilements.

While the buildings are well known for their simple yet picturesque appearance, the most important feature is their design. The sophistication of this design ensured the long term preservation the *Tripitaka* woodblocks by maintaining good ventilation, appropriate humidity levels, and an ideal temperature.

According to a study performed by Korean archeologists in 1996, the atmosphere inside the building remains at a relatively constant temperature (varying on average by 2°C), although it is a large wooden building (1,204.5m^2) without air conditioning or heating. Even when the outdoor temperature varies by more than 10°C, the temperature inside does not change by more than 5°C. The depositories are so well built that even if we were to construct a new storage building for the *Tripitaka* using the latest technology, we would not change the design.

The depository complex rests upon a granite foundation, and there is nothing apparently remarkable about the buildings themselves other than the two wooden latticework windows which appear in each wall. It is these wooden windows that hold the secret of preserving the *Tripitaka* woodblocks. Each wall has an upper and lower window, but the windows are different in size. In *Sudarajang*, the southern building of the depository complex, the lower windows of the front wall are four times larger than the upper windows. The upper windows of the back wall are 1.5 times larger than the lower windows.

In the northern building, known as the Dharma Jewel Hall, the lower windows of the front wall are 4.6 times larger than the upper windows. The upper windows in the back wall are 1.5 times larger than the lower windows.

These precise ratios demonstrate that the depository houses were built with an understanding of aerodynamics and its effect on storage conditions. The arrangement of the windows described above makes it possible to maximize

Depository Buildings at Haeinsa Temple

the natural flow of air. Thanks to the design, fresh air flows in naturally through the larger window, and fully circulates within the building before being let out through the windows on the opposite side.

The depository was built with mud walls and mud floors. These moderate the temperature during the hot summer and naturally keep humidity at a stable level. Beneath the mud floors of the depository chambers, we find several layers of charcoal, salt and limestone. These absorb excess moisture during the monsoon season, and release it during the dry winter when humidity levels fall.

The shelves on which the blocks are stored were made of thick, solid, squared lumber. Woodblocks are placed on the shelves like books, but in two layers, one on top of another. Since the end pieces of the woodblocks are thicker than the woodblocks themselves, the flow of air is naturally assisted when they are stored vertically, again helping to control humidity and temperature.

The excellent condition of the *Tripitaka Koreana* is something of a challenge to modern preservation techniques. Although the entire building is constructed with environmentally friendly materials, it serves its purpose better than any modern building.

In the 1960s, President Park Jung-hee ordered a new cement storage building to be made in the hills near Haeinsa Temple. The intention was to transfer the woodblocks to this new location in order to protect them from the danger of fire. However, when a small portion of the *Tripitaka* was moved to this storage building for a trial period, the woodblocks began to grow fungi. The ambitious plan to preserve the *Tripitaka* woodblocks through more "scientific" methods was abandoned.

Aside from the architectural advantages we have already discussed, certain aspects of the design and preservation capacity of the depository complex – such as the fact that insects and animals do not approach the buildings – remain unsolved mysteries. Since the founding of Haeinsa temple, there have been seven fires. The *Tripitaka Koreana* and the buildings in which they are stored have never been burned or damaged. Many Koreans, therefore, have believed that this was possible through the grace of the heavens, moved by the tireless devotion of their ancestors.

5. Hangul: Alphabet of Love

The perfect alphabet may be a hopelessly remote ideal, but it is possible to do a better job than history has made of the western alphabet, in any of its manifestations. We know this because there is an alphabet that is about as far along the road towards perfection as any alphabet is likely to get. Emerging in Korea in mid-fifteenth century, it has the status among language scholars normally reserved for classic works of art. In its simplicity, efficiency and elegance, this alphabet is alphabet's epitome, a star among alphabets, a national treasure for Koreans and "one of the great intellectual achievements of humankind", in the judgment of British linguist, Geoffrey Sampson.

–John Man, *Alpha Beta: How 26 Letters Shaped the Western World*

The Korean alphabet *Hangul*, which today has become a visual ambassador for Korean culture, was created in 1443 by King Sejong the Great (1397~1450). In 1446, it was set out in published form together with a manual explaining it in detail. Sejong named the alphabet and its accompanying volume *Hunmin Chongum* ("The proper Sounds for Instructing the People"). The Korean alphabet is nowadays commonly referred to as *Hangul*, which means the "Script of Han (Korea)" or the "Great Script."

Of the six thousand languages in existence today, only a hundred have their own alphabets. Of these one hundred languages, *Hangul* is the only alphabet made by an individual, for which the theory and motives behind its creation have been fully set out and explained. Roman characters have their origins in the hieroglyphics of Egypt and the syllabic Phoenician alphabets, and had to undergo a process of gradual evolution to become what they are today. Chinese characters, similarly, began as inscriptions on bones and tortoise shells, and took thousands of years to reach their current form.

However, *Hangul* is neither based on ancient written languages nor an imitation of another set of characters, but an alphabet unique to Korea. Moreover, as highly scientific writing system, based on profound linguistic knowledge and philosophical principles, *Hangul* is practical and convenient as well as beautiful. Its qualities have fascinated modern-day scholars around the world. Robert Ramsey, a professor at Maryland University, described the originality of *Hangul* as follows:

> The Korean alphabet is like no other writing system in the world. It is the only alphabet completely native to East Asia…The structure of the Korean alphabet shows a sophisticated understanding of phonological science that was not equaled in the West until modern times.

In his book *Writing Systems: A Linguistic Introduction*, British linguist Geoffrey Sampson devoted a special chapter to *Hangul*, and asserted:

> The history and theories of global writing systems have been raised to a new level with the advent of *Hangul*. Whether or not it is ultimately the best of all conceivable scripts for Korean, *Hangul* must unquestionably rank as one of the great intellectual achievements of humankind.

The praise of renowned scholars for this relatively young alphabet is seemingly endless. Professor Jared Diamond of UCLA, who won the Pulitzer Prize in

1997 for his book *Guns, Germs, and Steel,* wrote an article entitled "Writing Right" for the June 1994 edition of *Discover* magazine. In the article, he described *Hangul* as "an ultra-rational system" and "a precise reflection of a people's speech." Some other scholars even attribute Korea's rapid economic development and growth in information technology during recent decades to *Hangul,* which has helped to keep illiteracy rates in Korea among the lowest in the world.

The Principles of *Hangul*

For most of Korea's history, Koreans used ancient Chinese characters (*Hanja*) for writing. Since the tongues of the two nations belonged to different linguistic families, however, Korean was not ideally suited to be expressed in Chinese letters. In Chinese, for example, sentences are qualified with particles, whereas in Korean suffixes are used to add or modify meaning. Despite this inconvenience, the conservative Korean upper classes were firm in their support for its continued use.

There was a sudden change in the middle of the 15th century, initiated by a king who was both a scholar and a cultural pioneer. Through years of painstaking effort, King Sejong was able to analyze the basic units of medieval Korean speech using his own knowledge of linguistics, and finally succeeded in making it into an alphabet, called the *Hunmin Chongum*. An entry in the *Sejong Sillok* on 30th December in the 25th year of his reign shows that the new alphabet was Sejong's own invention: "This month the King has personally created 28 letters of *Onmun* [the vernacular script]... Though simple and concise, it is capable of infinite variations and is called *Hunmin Chongum*."

According to the *Explanations and Examples of the Hunmin Chongum*

(1446), the basic consonant symbols were schematic drawings of the human speech organs in the process of articulating certain sounds, while the other consonants were formed by adding strokes to these five basic shapes.

The velar ㄱ (k) depicts the root of the tongue blocking the throat.

The alveolar ㄴ (n) depicts the outline of the tongue touching the upper palate.

The labial ㅁ (m) depicts the outline of the mouth.

The dental ㅅ (s) depicts the outline of the incisor.

The laryngeal ㅇ (zero initial) depicts the outline of the throat.

The pronunciation of the aspirated velar ㅋ (k') is more forceful than that of ㄱ (k), and therefore a stroke is added.

CONSONANTS OF THE KOREAN ALPHABET

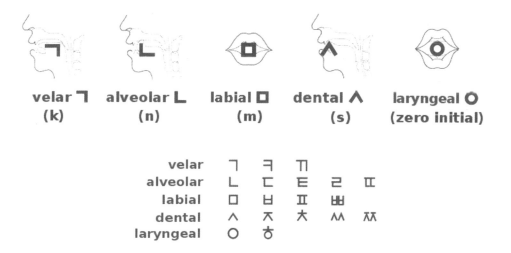

velar ㄱ	alveolar ㄴ	labial ㅁ	dental ㅅ	laryngeal ㅇ
(k)	(n)	(m)	(s)	(zero initial)

velar	ㄱ	ㅋ	ㄲ		
alveolar	ㄴ	ㄷ	ㅌ	ㄹ	ㄸ
labial	ㅁ	ㅂ	ㅍ	ㅃ	
dental	ㅅ	ㅈ	ㅊ	ㅆ	ㅉ
laryngeal	ㅇ	ㅎ			

31

The vowel symbols were formed according to the three fundamental symbols of Eastern philosophy.

The round ・ represents Heaven.
The flat ― represents Earth.
The upright ㅣ represents Man.

These three basic shapes are combined to derive other vowels: ㅏ, ㅑ, ㅓ, ㅕ, ㅗ. ㅛ. ㅜ, ㅠ. The consonants and vowels each represent a phoneme, or unit of speech, and together the letters make a syllable. For example, "Moon" in Korean is "달", which consists of: ㄷ (consonant)+ㅏ (vowel)+ㄹ (consonant). In other words, Korean is both a phonemic and a syllabic language.

G. K. Ledyard of Columbia University was deeply impressed by the scientific principles of the Korean alphabet. In his dissertation, *The Korean Language Reform of 1446*, he wrote as follows:

One of the most unique and interesting features of the Korean alphabet is the strict correspondence it shows between graphic shape and graphic function. Not only are the shapes of the consonants of a pattern different from those of the vowels, but even within these two main groups the shapes decided upon by Sejong clarify other important relationships...No other alphabet in the world is so beautifully, and sensibly, rational...It is really impossible to withhold admiration for this conception of a shape-function relationship and for the way it was carried out. There is nothing like it in all the long and varied history of writing. It would be quite enough merely to have the systematic shapes within

32

classes. But for those shapes themselves to be rationalized on the basis of the speech organs associated with their sounds — that is unparalleled grammatological luxury!

Founded on philosophical as well as scientific principles, *Hangul* embodies certain elements of the Confucian outlook. In traditional Eastern thought, *yin* stands for the concepts of feminine, passive, dark, dry and cold, while the *yang* encompasses the masculine, active, bright, humid and hot. From the interaction between these two principles arise the five elements of Wood, Fire, Earth, Metal and Water, which represent dynamic processes rather than physical entities. Corresponding to these principles, each vowel and consonant in *Hangul* is assigned the properties of either *yin* or *yang*, and the five basic consonants represent the five elements, according to their place of articulation.

The World's Most Advanced Alphabet

Most of the writing systems in the world today began as hieroglyphics (pictographs), eventually developing into ideographs, then syllabic characters, and finally phonemic alphabets.

The ancient Egyptian and Chinese characters were pictographs. Modern Chinese script, which evolved from pictographs, is the best-known ideograph, while the Japanese writing system is categorized as a syllabic alphabet. The most widely used alphabets in current times, the Roman (Latin) and Cyrillic characters, are phonemic, as is Greek, the mother alphabet of Roman and Cyrillic.

Hangul is commonly classed as a phonemic alphabet like the Roman and Cyrillic alphabets, but this is not strictly correct. *Hangul* is a unique alphabet in the sense that it has passed beyond the stage of phonemic characters. As explained above, "ㄱ" is a character in the shape of the root of the tongue blocking the throat. In other words, the Korean consonant has not only its own phoneme, but also its own "phoneme feature". Geoffrey Sampson, pointing out these characteristics of the Korean alphabet, has elevated *Hangul* to the status of a "featural alphabet." He concluded in his book that *Hangul* is the most developed alphabet in the entire history of written language.

Ignace Gelb, an American linguist, remarked in his book *A Study of Writing* that it took 1400 years for hieroglyphics to become syllabic characters and another 800 years for the syllabic characters to become alphabetic. The Korean alphabet bypassed 2200 years of development to reach the stage of the featural alphabet, one step beyond the phonemic alphabet. Thus it is no exaggeration to say that *Hangul* was a truly ground-breaking development in the history of written language.

An Alphabet of Compassion

The spoken language of our country is different from that of China and does not suit the Chinese characters. Therefore amongst uneducated people there have been many who, having something that they wish to put into words, have been unable to express their thoughts in writing. I am greatly distressed because of this, and so I have made twenty eight new letters. Let everyone practice them at their ease, and adapt them to their daily use.

–King Sejong's *Preface to Hunmin Chongum* (1446)

This passage, though short, demonstrates clearly the benevolent attitude of

King Sejong the Great, whose sincere hope was that all people should learn to read and write. Unfortunately, the circumstances were not favorable for his new invention.

A call for universal literacy was in King Sejong's day something of an anachronism. It would have been considered by many unnecessary and undesirable for the general population to be able to read. Some of those in power would even have thought it dangerous to put a tool as politically important as writing in the hands of the common people.

Nevertheless, King Sejong was very concerned about the education of his people. Not only did he often write about the importance of literacy, but he also urged those who had been educated to do their best to educate others, and encouraged women to learn how to read. While devoting himself to the creation of the Korean alphabet, Sejong almost lost his eyesight. With an illiteracy rate of almost zero in Korea today, the Korean people are still benefiting from the king's determination and self-sacrifice.

In memory of King Sejong's noble spirit, Koreans commemorate the *Hangul* Day every year on October 9th. UNESCO has also established the "King Sejong Literacy Prize", annually awarded to individuals or groups that have contributed greatly to the battle against global illiteracy.

Linguists of the world acknowledge the originality and depth of *Hangul*, and its logical and pragmatic basis. More valuable than the alphabet itself, however, is the selfless love and devotion of Sejong embodied within it. His sincere wish that all the people of his country could learn to express their thoughts in writing is the true pride of Korea and a spiritual heritage to share with the whole world.

6. King Sejong's Musical Notation

On 11 October 2006, a concert commemorating the 560th anniversary of the Korean alphabet was held in Yeakdang Hall at the National Center for Korean Traditional Performing Arts in Seoul. The concert featured the Court Music Memorial Orchestra, and was a re-enactment of the Royal Palace music of the 15th century. The programme included the *Yominrak* ("A Joy to Share with the People"), a composition of King Sejong the Great.

It is thanks to the musical notation devised by King Sejong that it is possible to recreate the Royal Palace Music today. The notation used was called *Chongganbo*. It consists of blocks of cells, each representing a unit of time, with the symbols of the notes written in each cell. If the name of a note appeared in two consecutive cells, the note would be played for twice as long; if two characters were written in one cell, they would be played twice as fast. A method of mensural notation, describing both the pitch and the length of a note, was unprecedented in the history of music. With the help of this new technique, it became possible to compose pieces for orchestra, before orchestral performances were known in the West.

During the same period in Europe, the neume system was being developed as a system of musical notation. It was created to represent the movement of melody, with notes moving up and down the page according to their pitch. The system was originally used as a mnemonic for reciting holy chants, and is still used today in the traditional music of the Eastern Orthodox Church. In its early stages, the neume system had no common standard and could not accurately represent the pitch and length of a note. By the 15th century, it had undergone various improvements, and was able to represent melodies with greater clarity. Passing through the hands of countless musicians, and after many alterations, it became established in the 17th century as the familiar five-line staff notation used today. It is therefore remarkable that a method of notation capable of recording both the pitch and length was developed in such a short span of time in Korea.

Thanks to the *Chongganbo,* many musical pieces of the early Choson period have survived, and have been enjoyed by Koreans over many centuries. The method of the *Chongganbo,* as it was originally conceived by King Sejong, has been passed down to us in the pages of the *Sejong Sillok,* and is still widely used in Korean music.

7. Sillok: The Royal Annals of the Choson Dynasty

The *Sillok*, or collected royal annals of the Choson period (1392~1910), is the world's most extensive record of a single dynasty, bringing together 472 years of history in a total of 1,893 volumes, from the first ruler, King Taejo, to the 25th, King Choljong.[3] While the annals of other nations were kept in manuscript form, those of the Choson dynasty were printed, and have survived to this day. The *Sillok* is therefore not only an extensive historical record, but also an expression of Korea's devotion to the preservation of history. The cultural and historical values of the *Sillok* were recognized from early on. It was designated as National Treasure No. 151 in 1973, and registered as part of UNESCO's "Memory of the World" in 1997.

The Task of Preserving History

Sillok literally means "a true and complete record." In the context of Korean history it refers to the official government archives, compiled by the state upon the death of a king. The court historians would meticulously record every event that occurred during a king's reign, and it was these records that

---

[3] The annals of the last two kings of Choson, Kojong and Sunjong, were published under Japanese direction during the occupation and are not generally included in the *Sillok*.

were assembled at the end to create the *Sillok*.

In order to make these records, the court historians followed the king every day, writing in shorthand every detail of his words and actions, conversations with ministers, meetings and their proceedings and so on. Political meetings held by the king were not open to all government officials. Permission to attend depended on the type of meeting and the official's rank. However, the court historians were free from all such restrictions. Wherever the king went, they would follow and record the discussions as they were held. The role of a court historian during the time of Choson was indeed highly privileged.

The first and foremost goal of the court historian was to record events plainly and objectively. It was believed that even kings should not be exempt from the judgment of history. The court historians, therefore, who were involved in every stage of preparing the *Sillok*, from recording to editing, were guaranteed independence and immunity in their tasks.

As the responsibilities of the court historians were very important, only young and competent officials were appointed to these full-time positions. A candidate was required to have passed the state literary examination with merit, and knowledge of literature and history were considered in addition to family background. A court historian was also required to be a person of great integrity, who would never compromise his principles when threatened with force, or even death. The aim of ensuring an accurate record of history was to enable future generations to benefit from the lessons of the past. There is an anecdote illustrating the rigor with which the historians of Choson fulfilled their duties.

In 1404, King Taejong fell from his horse during a hunting expedition. Embarrassed, looking to his left and right, he commanded, "Do not let the historian find out about this." To his disappointment, the historian accompanying the hunting party included these words in the annals, in addition to a description of the king's fall. The knowledge that their words and deeds would be documented in such a detailed manner, and judged by posterity, made kings fearful of history and served as a mechanism to curb tyrannical tendencies.

Upon the death of a king, the court historians would begin compiling the official *Sillok*, using their own day-to-day records, as well as the journals and reports of the main government offices and dispatches from officials posted throughout the land. The complete work would then be printed using movable type.

To ensure its preservation, four printed copies of the final *Sillok* were made. One was kept at the Royal Archive in the capital Seoul, the other three in the cities of Songju, Chongju and Chonju. This was a precaution against the annals being lost through fire, flooding, earthquake or other natural disasters. Even if one or two *Sillok* were lost, they could be restored using the copies stored in the other archives.

During the Imjin War (1592-1598), the whole nation was engulfed in conflict, and all four archives were at risk of being lost. The archives in Seoul, Songju and Chungju were all burned in the initial stages of the Japanese invasion. Fortunately, the remaining copy at the Chonju archive was moved to a remote hermitage in the mountains by local scholars directly before a planned Japanese raid, and two-hundred years of early Choson history were saved from calamity.

After the war, in spite of poor financial conditions, the Royal Court reprinted four copies using the surviving annals, and established four new depositories in remote mountain and island locations, in addition to the Royal Archive in Seoul. Thanks to these painstaking efforts, the *Sillok* annals that together cover the five hundred year history of Choson have been preserved to this day.

Restrictions on Viewing the *Sillok*

Even today, there are certain state documents which remain classified or are publicly released only after a certain period of time. Some particularly sensitive documents may be released only after several decades, when their disclosure will not cause any undue disturbance. The same principle was followed with the *Sillok*.

The purpose of the *Sillok* was to pass on the lessons of history to future generations. An objective, unaltered account was therefore of vital importance, and for this reason no one besides the court historians had free access either to the daily records or the completed *Sillok* itself. After several generations had passed, certain other people were allowed to read the *Sillok*, but even then only by permission of the court historians. Even kings were not exempt from this rule.

In the case of China, where the authority of the monarch was much stronger, the king would often read the official state records in spite of opposition from his ministers. And because they were open to be read by the king, the annals of China could not avoid being compromised. Fearing the consequences, the historians felt compelled to write according to the king's wishes, and so often put circumlocution before candor. In Choson dynasty Korea, however, the rule that not even the king was allowed to read the annals was observed almost without exception.

King Sejong the Great, who was deeply devoted to his parents, wanted to read the annals of his father Taejong's reign. He was curious to know how the historians had evaluated and recorded his father's acts in government. Due to fierce opposition from his ministers, however, Sejong did not read the records in the end. Here is the entry in the *Sejong Sillok* which records the episode:

The King said,

"Now that the *Taejong Sillok* has been completed, I wish to read it for myself. What is your opinion?"

The Vice-Prime Minister Maeng Sa-song replied,

"If Your Majesty reads the *Sillok* now, future kings will wish to do the same. And if the king who reads the *Sillok* is displeased by what he sees, he will try to make changes to it, and so the royal historians will not be able to record history in its wholeness, fearing the King's punishment. In that case, Your Majesty, how can the truth of history be preserved for future generations?"

The King replied, "What you say is true."

– Sejong Sillok, 20th March, 13th year of Sejong's reign

This story of how King Sejong wished to read the *Sillok*, but bowed to the advice of his ministers, served as an important precedent throughout Choson period. When the kings of subsequent generations requested to read the annals of recent times, the ministers would cite the example of King Sejong, and so dissuade the king from reading it.

An Achievement in World Government History

State annals are found in the other countries of East Asia, but in terms of extensiveness and detail, as well as richness of content, there are few that equal the Choson-period *Sillok* of Korea. Japan has the annals of certain rulers before the 10th century, and Vietnam has records for the 150 years between 1802 and 1945. In the case of China, while the annals of the Ming and the Qing dynasties contain records of 260 and 296 years respectively, each falls short of the years covered by the *Sillok* of the Choson dynasty, which documents 472 years.

Of the various government records of Asia, the one closest to the *Sillok* of Korea in terms of age, style and ideology is that of Ming China. The Ming annals, however, do not cover the entire history of the dynasty, and only thirteen out of the sixteen imperial reigns are documented. In terms of size, the Ming Chinese annals have 16 million words, while the Choson Korean annals contain 47 million – three times as many.

When we compare the records of diplomatic exchanges between Choson Korea (1392~1910) and Ming China (1368~1644), it is again apparent from the overlapping parts of the annals that the Choson dynasty *Sillok* is far more detailed. In the accounts of relations between the two dynasties, all the incidents recorded in the Ming annals can be found in the Choson annals, whereas not all of those mentioned in the Choson annals are found in the Ming annals.

The detailed account of interactions between nations in East Asia, and in particular the diplomatic relations between the dynasties, which we find in the Choson *Sillok*, have long been recognized by academics worldwide as being of great historical importance. As a factual source of information about Manchuria, a former territory of Korea and for a long time home to various nomadic tribes, the Choson *Sillok* is well known to the historians of China and Japan, as well as scholars in the West.

Contribution to the Study of World History

The multi-volume *Sillok* is a treasure trove of historical and cultural information relating to 500 years of Choson history. As well as addressing subjects such as politics, diplomacy, military, civil affairs, law, economics and transport, it also covers astronomy, geography and music, making it something of an encyclopedia. Worthy of its place in the "Memory of the World" programme, the *Sillok* also provides an invaluable insight into the culture and history of other nations in East Asia.

The scope of the annals of the Choson dynasty extends even beyond East Asia. Though the fruits of worldwide research based on the *Sillok* have been limited to date, one rewarding example is the study of Professor Lee Tae-jin of Seoul National University, entitled "The Little Ice Age of the 17th Century."

In a series of papers based on the recordings of the annals, Lee claims that for 250 years, between 1500 and 1750, Earth experienced a series of extreme weather patterns following a large meteorite impact, the most serious of which was the onset of colder temperatures. Classifying this as a miniature Ice Age, he demonstrates that the course of history was significantly influenced by these unusual conditions. The transition of Chinese dynasties in 1664, and the widespread political instability of the early 17th century throughout Asia, Europe and America, are all shown to have occurred during this period.

Professor Lee's investigations were based almost entirely on the astronomical and meteorological records he found in the annals of the Choson dynasty, as there was no historical record in the world that could equal them in this particular line of research. Despite their many volumes, the annals of Ming and Qing dynasties contain only brief references to astronomy and natural phenomena. Under the powerful royal authority, it was difficult to record such natural phenomena in China openly. According to Confucian beliefs, unusual phenomena in nature or the skies were directly construed as a sign of misgovernment by the ruler, and therefore details of these phenomena were generally omitted from the official Chinese records. Moreover, amid the turmoil during the period of transition from the Ming dynasty to the new Qing dynasty, continuity and consistency in such observational records could hardly be maintained. In Europe also during this period, it was not yet possible to conduct astronomical studies independently of the religious authorities.

History in the Digital Age

As a result of ambitious projects to translate the *Sillok* into modern Korean, and to convert it into digital format, public availability of the archive is being made possible on a scale far greater than any other pre-modern records in East Asia.

Because the vast volumes of the *Sillok* were originally written in ancient Chinese characters (Chinese being the traditional written language of scholars and officials), even though they were technically available to all, they were not directly accessible even to many scholars. In order to reach a wider audience, it was necessary to translate the ancient Chinese characters into modern Korean. Since the annals contain countless technical words used across numerous specialist fields, the translation process was by no means straightforward. Completed in 1993, it took 26 years to translate all 1,893 original volumes. It was a colossal achievement, which opened up the royal annals to scholars of various fields and also the general public, previously prevented by the language barrier from reading the work.

To improve access to the vast collection further, the annals of Choson were published in CD-ROM format for the first time in 1995. Since 2005, both the original and the translated version have been available online at http://sillok.history.go.kr. This online database is fully indexed, and searchable by subject or keyword. The potential for an individual to access a vast library of his own nation's historical literature at home, to read and research at any time, may sound like a dream to the scholars of other nations. Anyone who is interested can freely peruse the annals of Choson dynasty and enter into its history and culture.

Dr. James Lewis, a lecturer in Korean History at Oxford University, once paid a visit to a colleague in Japan, who was studying late Choson economic history. Lewis had collected all the records relating to a particular law using the CD-ROM of the *Sillok*, and put the records on two floppy disks. As he gave the diskettes to his friend and explained the contents, the friend stood still for a moment looking at them, and then became excited, almost laughing and crying at the same time. It turned out that it had taken Dr. Lewis only three hours to do what his friend had achieved in three years.

The recent growth in the publication of books about the Choson dynasty, and the huge popularity of movies and TV dramas set in the Choson period, both in Korea and abroad, can be attributed to the popularization of the *Sillok* through digital media. In this respect, *Sillok* has served as a cultural bridge linking the past to the present, and Korea to the wider world.

8. Diaries of the Royal Secretariat

The Diaries of the Royal Secretariat refer to the journals written by the *Sungjongwon*, or Secretariat to the King, in the Choson period (1392~1910). It is likely that these diaries were written from the very beginning of the dynasty, although only the last 288 years have survived (1623~1910). Unlike the royal annals of *Sillok*, which were replicated and stored in four different archives, the diaries were kept only in the offices of the Secretariat inside the palace, and during the Japanese Invasion (1592~1598) and the Revolt of Yi Kwal (1642), these and all other records stored in the palace were destroyed by fire.

Despite the loss of these earlier volumes, the *Diaries* are the world's most voluminous chronological record in history, comprising some 240 million characters in 3,245 volumes, five times larger than the *Sillok* of 47 million characters in 1,893 volumes. In recognition of their historic value, the *Diaries of the Royal Secretariat* were designated as Korea's National Treasure No. 303 in April 1999, and included in UNESCO's "Memory of the World" register in September 2001.

The fact that two public chronicles from the same era – the *Sillok* and the *Diaries* – are registered in the "Memory of the World" programme is testimony to the eminence of Korea's documentary tradition. As a French navy officer was surprised to discover after an attack on Kanghwa Island in 1886, all Koreans of the Choson period, even the poorest, lived in companionship with books. Owing to this cultured environment, a rich and vast legacy of literary works was written and passed down to subsequent generations. Besides official records such as the *Sillok* and *Diaries of the Royal Secretariat*, it was customary for scholars to publish monographs and anthologies containing their own reflections and compositions, and many of these diverse historical documents and writings have survived from the time of Choson.

The Royal Secretariat, or *Sungjongwon*, was responsible for communicating royal commands and instructions to the relevant government departments and local officials throughout the country. The Secretariat also relayed to the king reports intended for his attention, submissions made by ministers and so on. It also engaged extensively in the administration of the state, including the preparation of receptions for foreign envoys, as well as ceremonies like the royal ancestral rites. The implementation of executive orders, selection of personnel, and the holding of official state examinations were amongst its other responsibilities.

It was the function of the members of the Secretariat to attend the King closely, and so the *Diaries* are much more detailed than the *Sillok* in their description of events that directly concerned the monarch. For example, an entry in the *Sillok* on 14th November, in the 46th year of King Yongjo's reign (1770), briefly mentions an order from the king that "Unpaid taxes to the value of 40 thousand sacks of grain are to remain uncollected throughout the nation." The entry in the *Diaries* on the same day gives a complete account of the circumstances of the order. King Yongjo, whose health was declining due to old age, had his pulse examined by the royal physicians, and his condition was diagnosed as normal. To show his gratitude, he was seeking to return the grace of the heavens by rewarding the people, and when his Prime Minister proposed a cancellation of the grain-taxes, the king held a discussion and the proposal was accepted. A month of such entries, recorded on a daily basis, were compiled and presented to the king for his approval before the 20th of every month, after which the record was stored in the office of the Royal Secretariat.

Since they were based mainly on the reports of the members of the Secretariat, who served as aides to the king, the *Diaries* did not cover everything. Episodes unrelated to the king, or which took place in other areas of the kingdom, are better documented in the *Sillok*. For example, we find a more detailed account of the crown prince's admission to school on 11th March in the *Sunjo Sillok* than in the *Diaries*. Descriptions of natural disasters which affected the whole country, such as floods and earthquakes, are much more detailed in the *Sillok*, which incorporated extensive reports from each of the local governments. Consequently, the value of the *Diaries* as a historical source is greatly enhanced if it is read in conjunction with the *Sillok*.

The *Diaries* also made a careful record of the weather, with entries such as "morning rain, evening clear," and "morning sunny, afternoon cloudy," appearing daily for 288 years. Whenever there was rainfall, the amount of precipitation was measured using a rain gauge and duly recorded. It has been remarked that the weather observations contained in the *Diaries* could by themselves contribute greatly to an understanding of meteorology from 17th century to the early 20th century.

Just as the significance of the *Royal Sillok* lies in its uninterrupted account of 472 years of history, the *Diaries*, although beginning in 1623, are an important part of Korea's documentary tradition, continuously recording 288 years of its past, on a scale greater than any other historical record in the world.

9. Uigwe: Colorful Documentary Heritage

Another item of Korea's past that illustrates its dedication to recording history is the *Uigwe*. The term *Uigwe* was formed by combining the two words *uisik* (ceremony) and *gwebum* (example), and it refers to a class of books which described in detail, using visual illustration as well as words, the major events or tasks undertaken by the state or the royal family of the Choson dynasty (1392~1910). Since it was customary to follow the precedents set by previous kings when events of national importance were held, the procedures were documented comprehensively in *Uigwe* in order to serve as a guide for future generations. Characteristic of Korea's colorful documentary heritage, the *Uigwe* has been recognized as significant by many scholars in the world, and was included in the "Memory of the World" register in June 2007.

There are as many kinds of *Uigwe* as there were national events and ceremonies in Choson Korea. These included the royal wedding, palace banquets, investitures, coronations, funerals and ancestral rites for the royal family. *Uigwe* were also compiled in the case of the publication of important works of literature, such as the *Sillok*, and also the construction of palaces and fortresses.

In their accounts of royal functions such as weddings and funerals, not only the order of events, the participants and their personal attributes were recorded. Even the size, color, and constituent parts of the items used in the ceremony were closely documented with accompanying illustrations.

Records which concerned the building of palaces and fortifications included a description of the building's location, its structure and layout, the materials used in the building process, the budgeted and actual expenditures of the project, and the daily progress of the construction work. In recording the names of everyone who participated in the project, from the director-in-chief to the servants and laborers, it instilled a sense of pride and responsibility in all who contributed.

The documentation was so thorough and complete that any recorded ceremony can be perfectly re-enacted, and any major building of the Choson period reconstructed without difficulty.

Detail from an eight-paneled *Uigwe* screen entitled "Royal Procession to the Ancestral Tomb in Hwaseong" 18th century, color on silk, H 142.0cm W 62.0cm, Samsung Museum of Art

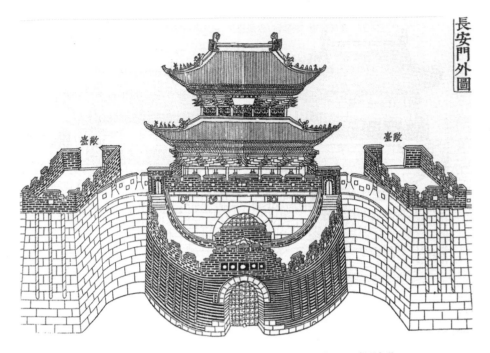

A page from *Hwaseong Fortress Uigwe* (1796)

Hwaseong Fortress, for example, designated as part of the World Heritage by UNESCO, was originally built in the 18th century and was reduced to ruins during the Korean War (1950). Thanks to the *Hwaseong Fortress Uigwe*, however, it was possible to restore it perfectly during the 1970s.

For a historic building to receive due recognition by UNESCO, in addition to its historic and artistic value, its authenticity and state of preservation are very important. If the original appearance of the building is lost during repair or reconstruction, this would be regarded as a critical flaw. Therefore, when the UNESCO inspectors came to examine the Hwaseong Fortress to consider its registration in the World Heritage, their primary concern was whether it had been faithfully restored to its original state. Upon seeing the *Hwaseong Fortress Uigwe* (1796), an exhaustive eight-volume report documenting the original construction of the fortress, it is said that the UNESCO inspectors could not hold back their astonishment at the amount of information and level of detail. Since the *Hwaseong Fortress Uigwe* had been followed to the letter in the reconstruction process, the inspectors were unable to find any flaws in the restoration of the fortress, and in 1977 its registration was complete.

Another notable feature of the records is their rich illustrations. Together with paintings that depict the various stages of a ceremony, diagrams of the buildings and articles used are all included in *Uigwe* without exception. The materials used to make these pictures and illustrations are also recorded, and most are natural ingredients such as plants and minerals. Even after hundreds of years, the pictures in the *Uigwe* have not been discolored, and still exhibit the vivid yet calm shades unique to natural colorings. It is clear that the use of these organic pigments ensured the preservation of original colorings. Thanks to the illustrations, one can go back several hundreds of years to relive a ceremony as it was performed at the time, and thus better understand the more precise details that could not have been perceived simply by reading the text.

Accurately portraying the life of the Royal Court and the majestic national ceremonies from hundreds of years ago, *Uigwe* is an ideal source for scholars studying the traditions of Korean royalty. Academics specializing in traditional clothing carefully note the dress and ornaments worn in the pictures of the *Uigwe*, and those studying the royal cuisine pay close attention to the various dishes which appear on the banquet tables, as well as their recipes. Researchers in traditional music can examine the works played at the different ceremonies, their orchestration and the diagrams of the musical instruments used. For those studying the history of architecture, it is possible to analyze the structure of buildings and the raw materials used to make them in detail.

Besides all this, the records of the *Uigwe* give us a deeper understanding of the government system of Choson-period Korea, and how each of the departments functioned at different points in history. Through the records of taxes, wages paid to employees and expenditure on goods and provisions, they also give us an insight into the history of currency.

Perhaps the most important legacy of *Uigwe* is its testimony to the dedication of the ancestors to an accurate and meticulous documentation of history. By recording in *Uigwe* the important events of the state in such minute detail, down to the use of a single coin or nail, and ensuring that they were publicly disclosed, the possibility that public funds might be embezzled or wasted was removed from the outset.

Normally, fewer than a dozen copies of *Uigwe* were made after each national ceremony. Of these, the first copy, which required the most effort to prepare, was presented to the king, and the rest were distributed to the office in charge of state protocol, the archives in Seoul and offices in other regions. For the Royal *Uigwe* offered to the sovereign, a much higher quality of paper was used than for the other copies, its covers were made of silk, and a brass binding and chrysanthemum-shaped decorations were added. When the French Navy invaded the Kanghwa Island in 1886 and came across a store of Royal *Uigwe* in the archives, they were enchanted by their elegance and beauty, and carried the 297 volumes they had found back to France.

The greatest collection of *Uigwe* is currently at Seoul National University. It consists of 560 different kinds of *Uigwe*, amounting to 3,000 volumes in total. The Academy of Korean Studies in Seoul houses another collection which contains 300 different varieties and 500 volumes in total. The 297 volumes taken by the French in 1886 are kept at the National Library of France, and a further 69 varieties of *Uigwe,* taken to Japan during the colonial period, are kept at the Imperial Household Agency in Kyoto.

Part Two
Fine Art

10. Golden Crowns of Silla

The Chronicles of Japan (AD 720), a work published by royal decree during the Nara period in Japan, contains the following description: "A country that is filled with the splendor of gold and silver, such is the kingdom of Silla." Similar accounts are found in records from as far afield as the Middle East. In his *Book of Creation and of History* (AD 996), an Arab historian remarked, "Silla people decorate their houses with silk interwoven with golden thread, and use golden plates and cutlery at meals." Al-Idrisi, another Arab traveler, recorded that "Gold is so commonplace in Silla that the people use it to make chains for dogs and collars for monkeys."

As these historic records indicate, the ancient Korean kingdom of Silla (BC 57~AD 935) was a country in which many gold works of art were produced, and its advanced technology and craftsmanship won the admiration of other countries. The golden crowns of Silla are the foremost examples of its expertise.

Though they are now regarded as symbolic of ancient Korean art, it has been less than a hundred years since the golden crowns of Silla were first discovered, drawing the attention of the world with their exquisite beauty and delicate design. After the first crown was found at Kumgwan Tomb in 1921, others were discovered at the tombs of Kumryong, Sobong and Chonma, and the Great Tomb at Hwangnam. A crown buried in a tomb at Kyodong in Kyongju was later rediscovered, having been stolen by a grave robber. The crowns have been found in royal tombs dating from the 5th and early 6th centuries, and all were

Gold Crown from Hwangnam Great Tomb

5-6th century AD, H 27.5cm, National Treasure No. 191, Seoul National Museum

made of pure gold.

Scholars estimate that there are about 150 large tombs in and around the city of Kyongju, the ancient capital of Silla kingdom. Since only around thirty of these have been excavated, it is unknown how many more gold crowns may yet be found. There are only about ten crowns of pure gold from ancient times which survive in the world today. Six of these are from the kingdom of Silla and two from Kaya, another ancient Korean kingdom. Most of the crowns in the other kingdoms of East Asia at the time were not made of gold, but gilt-bronze. It is no wonder that the spectacular crowns of Silla have been recognized as among the most valuable findings in East Asian archeology.

The basic frame of a gold crown is in the shape of a tree branch or antler. This is due to the respect and wonder that the people of ancient times felt towards nature. A tree spreads its roots deep in the earth, yet its branches reach toward the heavens. It was therefore believed to represent a link between the heavens and the earth. A tree was also believed to symbolize eternal life, since it eternally rejuvenates itself. The reindeer, also known as "the gentleman of the forest" in ancient shamanistic culture, was considered to be sacred as well. For many centuries, the reindeer appeared in paintings, folding screens, and decorations on furniture as one of the Ten Symbols of Longevity.

To the basic structure of the crown, hundreds of golden orbs were affixed by means of tiny, twisted golden wires. Even the slightest movement caused these ornaments to shimmer like stars. Fashioned jewels made out of jade, known as *kok-ok* in Korean, were placed in between them, so the radiant color would be more noticeable, like jade leaves moving in a golden forest.

The jade jewel resembles an embryo, and symbolized fertility, abundance, and continuity of life. In ancient Greece, this shape represented an eggplant, which was known to spread its seeds well. These jewels were also attached to the crown loosely, so that when the person wearing the crown moved, both the jade and golden ornaments would have an audible effect as well as a visual one.

The only other ancient crowns of pure gold were made by the Sarmatians near the Black Sea and the Tillia Tepe of present-day Afghanistan, and were

Gold Crown from Chonma Tomb

5-6th century AD, H 32.5cm, National Treasure No. 188, Kyongju National Museum

produced a few centuries before the Silla crowns. The unique artistry and intricate decorations of the golden crowns of Silla, however, leave them truly without equal.

11. Golden Earrings of Silla

In Kyongju, capital of the Silla kingdom that prospered for about a millennium (BC 57~AD 935), numerous relics of its ancient past can still be found throughout the city, giving it the appearance of a huge museum without walls. The ancient tombs, which protrude from the ground here and there like small hills, are the most noticeable signs of its long history. Many luxurious gold artifacts such as crowns, necklaces, rings, belts and shoes have been unearthed from these tombs, along with other items including pottery and works of glass and bronze.

The tombs of Kyongju have yielded some of the world's most splendid ancient treasures. From the mound of Chonma alone, more than 10,000 items were excavated in 1973. These included jewelry and personal accessories, weaponry, cavalry gear, and tableware. Amongst these, the golden earrings are believed to be the greatest examples of the high aesthetics and skillful metal craftsmanship of the ancient Silla people, together with the golden crowns. In world archaeology and art history, they are first to be mentioned in any discussion of ancient earrings, and are seen as the finest of their kind.

The gold earrings of this period are called *taehwan* (thick earrings) or *sehwan* (thin earrings), depending on the thickness of the upper ring. Earrings of both kinds became more sophisticated and varied in shape as time went on. The earrings of the 6th century in particular have remarkably delicate designs, often decorated with hundreds of tiny gold granules and green or red pieces of

Silla Gold Earrings
6th century AD,
Excavated in Kyesong,
Kimhae National
Museum

jade.

In the case of *taehwan* earrings, the diameter of the upper ring is 3.5cm, while the overall length of the earring is 9cm or more. Many accessories are attached to this upper ring by means of a second ring below, making the earrings appear heavy. In fact, the inside of the upper ring is hollow, and it is lighter than it appears. *Taehwan* earrings are believed to have been hung from a gold crown or silk hat as ornaments, rather than worn directly on the ears. In the case of *sehwan*, the ring is not hollow, but solid. Earrings were usually worn by men as well as women in ancient Korea. Men wore the thinner *sehwan* earrings and women the thicker *taehwan*.

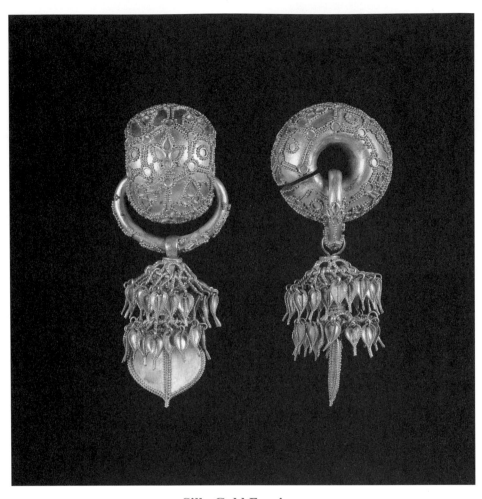

Silla Gold Earrings

6th century AD, Length 8.7cm, Seoul National Museum

The gold earrings shown above were excavated from a tomb in Pomun-dong, Kyongju. They are considered to be the most beautiful and elaborate earrings discovered in the Silla tombs so far.

On the upper rings, which have a diameter of 3.5cm, the hexagon-shaped back of a turtle is traced out with scores of gold granules, each with a diameter of 0.7mm, and thin gold threads. Within these patterns, we find arrangements of three or four leaves. The smaller ring, which connects the upper ring to the lower section, is also decorated with a leaf design, again using gold granules. Other gold earrings of a similar kind generally have between 18 and 24 hanging ornaments in the lower section, but these have 37. The rims and borders of all these accessories are studded with golden granules. In total, there are 5000 gold granules on each earring. They represent the culmination of centuries of gold craftsmanship.

This technique of decorating items with gold granules and gold thread can be seen in the metalwork of the ancient Greeks, and the technique presumably spread via Central Asia and China to Korea. Silla artisans refined the technique to make objects of great delicacy, not emulated by other nations. The technique travelled from Korea across the East Sea to Japan, and had a visible influence on its craftsmanship. Earrings similar to those of the Silla kingdom are occasionally found in Japanese tombs from the 4th century to the early 7th century.

The culture of gold that flourished during the Silla period reached its zenith in the 5th and 6th centuries, and underwent a significant change when Buddhism was introduced to Korea. The practice of erecting opulent *tumuli* in the capital Kyongju and neighboring areas steadily declined, and the burial of golden relics with the dead all but ceased. The brilliant workmanship of Silla that had formerly been dedicated to the king and queen was reborn, and now manifested itself in Buddhist art, such as Buddha statues and *sarira* reliquaries. The next chapter will discuss the famous *sarira* reliquary of the Kamunsa Temple, often referred to as the highest achievement in reliquary art.

12. The Sarira Reliquary of Kamunsa Temple

In a traditional Buddhist temple, the two most important buildings were the prayer hall, which enshrined the statue of Buddha, and the pagoda. Originally, the pagoda symbolized the Buddha's tomb, as it enshrined Buddha's *sarira* – marble-like relics which remain after the cremation of an enlightened being.

After the Shakyamuni Buddha entered nirvana, the *sarira* were distributed among the eight ancient kingdoms of India. Subsequently, King Ashoka, the third king of the Maurya dynasty, retrieved seven of these eight *sarira* and distributed them throughout the world.

In AD 546, the Buddha's *sarira* were first introduced to Korea. When he beheld the *sarira*, King Chinhung of the Silla dynasty renounced the world and became a Buddhist monk. As this shows, the Buddha's *sarira* were greatly revered, and might awaken great faith, even in a king, to renounce the secular world.

However, since the Buddha's *sarira* were limited in number, people began to enshrine Buddhist sutras in pagodas instead. Whether they enshrined the *sarira* that represented the Buddha's body or the sutras that represented the Buddha's spirit, the pagodas were treated as sacred and precious objects of worship.

The first pagodas in India were dome-shaped tombs called *stupas*. As Buddhism spread to other countries, the form of the pagoda changed, and different materials such as stone, brick, metal, and wood were used to build it. In every country, great efforts were taken to make the shrine of the Buddha's relics as beautiful and elaborate as possible.

The Stone Pagoda – Buddha's Palace

On the outskirts of Kyongju city, the ancient capital of Silla, lie the ruins of a 1300 year-old temple. Currently only two pagodas of the original temple buildings survive. The Buddhist King Munmu (AD 626~681) accomplished the difficult task of unifying the three ancient Korean kingdoms (Koguryo, Paekche and Silla) through his great faith and devotion. He then began to build a temple in Kyongju in order to protect the country from the invasions of Japanese pirates, which were growing worse by the day. However, he did not live to witness the completion of the temple. The responsibility passed to his son Sinmun, who completed it in AD 682, and named the temple Kamunsa, which means "in gratitude for grace."

The Kamunsa temple overlooks the East Sea, where the tomb of King Munmu lies. This tomb is also known as the "Rock of the Great King". Before he passed away, King Munmu declared, "When I die, I will become a dragon that will protect this country from the invading enemy. Therefore, let me be buried in the sea." According to this wish, his subjects built him a tomb in the waters of the East Sea. The main Buddha hall of the Kamunsa temple was designed so that the sea water could enter beneath the building. This was to allow the king, who had become a dragon, to visit this temple freely.

In 1996, over 1300 years later, when the Kamunsa temple's Eastern Pagoda was taken apart for repairs, an astonishing discovery was made in the form of a delicate and masterfully crafted *sarira* reliquary, the like of which had not been seen before anywhere in the world.

A *sarira* reliquary is a work of art that is made for the purpose of holding the relics of a Buddha or a Buddhist master. Since the objects it contains are considered sacred, the reliquary is made to enshrine them, using the greatest artistic skill and most advanced techniques of the day, so that it will be both exquisite and robust. This is true of all *sarira* reliquaries, including those of India, where they originated, and in other countries where Buddhism was adopted, such as China and Japan. The *sarira* reliquary of Kamunsa Temple, however, has received particular attention for its unparalleled beauty and craftsmanship.

The reliquary consists of an inner and an outer container. The outer container is embossed with four devas on each side, and the inner container is decorated with intricate designs and ornamentation.

The inner container represents the Prayer Hall of a Buddhist temple. The intention of the artisans was to enshrine Buddha in a palace, since Buddha's *sarira* represent the Buddha himself. The reliquary, however, was not created simply to house the *sarira*. It was also intended to depict a miniature version of the Buddha's Pure Land. According to Dr. Shin Dae-hyun, a scholar of Buddhist art, such profound symbolism is not found in other *sarira* reliquaries. The subtle artistry and pious devotion of the vessel's design often comes as a surprise to modern people.

The Elaborate Design of the Sarira Reliquary

The outer container of the *sarira* reliquary is in the shape of a simple box, standing about 30cm tall. The four Devas embossed on each side look so vivid that they seem about to come alive. As guardian deities, they are wearing armor, which appears to be covered with scales, and hold weapons in their hands.

Their faces are animated, with vibrant eyes, lifelike mustaches and lines

Inner Container of the Kamunsa Temple *Sarira* Reliquary

7th century AD, H 18.8cm, Gilt-bronze, Seoul National Museum

etched on their foreheads. The hair looks as if it has just been combed, and even the creases on their open palms can be seen.

The images of the Devas were made by hammering metal plate. The more detailed aspects of the design must have required more complex procedures. They were fixed to the surface of the outer container with small copper nails.

A full examination of the reliquary has shown that the outer walls were made of copper plated with gold. This gold layer has survived intact to this day. It has been established that this is because the outer container was gilded no fewer than four times by the craftsmen.

In order to produce gold layering, small pieces of gold must be ground to tiny granules. These granules are then mixed with mercury. The mixture is ground further, and then wrapped in paper and compressed tightly to squeeze the mercury out. The remainder is then evenly applied to the surface of the metal by hand. When the metal is heated, the remaining traces of mercury evaporate and the gold remains strongly attached to the metal surface. Because of the efforts of the artisans of ancient Korea, who repeated this process four times, the four Devas of the *sarira* reliquary have been able to retain their splendid appearance for 1300 years.

Once the outer container is opened, the inner container, crafted in the image of the Heavens, reveals itself. Although it is intricately detailed, it is only 18.8cm tall, no more than the span of a palm. The base portion is guarded by four lions, each with unique facial features. The four sides of the base section are decorated with carved images of bodhisattvas and other divinities. Even the background to these images is filled with detail.

The upper section of the inner container is surrounded by fences and a gate, and covered by a lattice roof. In the centre of the enclosure there is an urn in the shape of a lotus flower, with four Devas and four monks standing guard around it. Their faces, each the size of a grain of rice, have been given distinct expressions.

The roof portion that covers the *sarira* reliquary is decorated with many ornaments, such as goddesses, bells, and the images of Bodhisattvas. The most notable of all these ornaments is the wind chime. It is about 0.04g in weight, almost undetectable to human senses. The main body of the bell was made with thin gold plate, 0.1mm thick. The chain which connected the bell to the roof was as thick as a strand of a hair.

When the wind chime is magnified 200 times using a microscope, we find three gold granules, each 0.3mm in diameter, soldered on to its surface. Even modern artisans who specialize in recreating ancient works of art are amazed by this achievement. How was it possible to make these 0.3mm gold granules, which can barely be seen with naked eye?

First, a thin gold thread was taken, and cut into tiny pieces of uniform length. When these pieces were heated at a high temperature, they became sphere-shaped granules, due to surface tension. Three granules were then grouped together and solder was placed in between them. The solder consisted of 90% gold and 10% silver. When heat was applied, the solder, having a lower melting point than pure gold, melted first and attached the gold granules to the metal surface.

The melting points of the gold and the solder differed by about 20 degrees. It is unknown how the ancient artisans were aware of this difference and able to take it into account, considering that they did not have modern heating equipment (they are believed to have used charcoal).

The pieces of solder were also kept to as small a size as possible, which meant that each granule could retain its round appearance, without any noticeable trace of the solder being left behind. Through examining the minute artistry of the wind chime, we can see how the ancient artisans devoted all their skill to parts of the reliquary which could not even be seen.

In 2002, a KBS history documentary team carried out an experiment, their

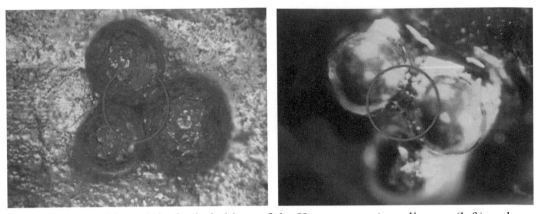

Comparison of the original wind chime of the Kamunsa *sarira* reliquary (left) and a replica by a modern artisan (right).

goal being to replicate the wind chime of the Kamunsa *sarira* reliquary. A distinguished modern artisan, who was an expert in restoring ancient artifacts, was asked to make a copy of the wind chime, including the feature of three 0.3mm gold granules. Although he had the benefit of modern heating equipments, the results show the original wind chime is more elegant and better made, with no trace of solder showing between the granules, in contrast to the modern reproduction which shows clear signs of soldering. The pictures above are magnified 200 times.

The Many Layers which Enshrined the Buddha

A total of 54 *sarira* were recovered from the Kamunsa Temple reliquary. The container which actually held the relics was a crystal bottle. It was about 3.65cm in height, slightly shorter than a match stick. The golden lid that covered this crystal bottle was 1.2cm in diameter, with a dense covering of 0.3mm gold granules, all soldered on in the same fashion as those found on the wind chime.

The crystal bottle that contained the *sarira* was stored within an urn in the shape of a lotus flower, and the urn was placed in the center of the inner container. The gilt-bronze outer container was added in order to protect it, and the huge pagoda was built to enshrine the reliquary itself. These many layers of art work showed how they truly revered the *sarira* as the body of Buddha, and wanted to protect it.

In this tiny relic, we can see the high level of technological development in ancient Korea, as well as the noble spirit of its people, who hoped to protect the teachings of Buddha and to defend the country from foreign invasion.

13. The Gilt-Bronze Incense Burner of Paekche

On December 12, 1993, between the fortress walls and the tombs of the ancient Paekche Kingdom (BC 18~AD 660), one of the most extraordinary archeological discoveries of the 20th century was made. Developers were planning to build a parking lot on a stretch of abandoned farmland, to be used by tourists visiting the ancient tombs. While they were surveying the site prior to construction, they unexpectedly came across a remarkable incense burner from the time of ancient Paekche, stored inside the remains of a wooden container used in a temple forge for cooling metal.

The body and lid of the incense burner were discovered separately, and both were in such good condition that it was hard to believe they had been underground for over 1300 years. It is possible that the incense burner was hurriedly stored in the wooden container during times of trouble (Paekche was invaded and overthrown by Silla in AD 660), and remained there until it was discovered in 1993. This explanation is supported by the fact that the burner was not found with a separate container for carrying the incense. In the April of the year following its discovery, Seoul National Museum put on a special exhibition, with the incense burner as the sole exhibit. The exhibition lasted for twelve days, during which time sixty-eight thousand people visited the museum in order to catch a glimpse of the newly-found treasure.

Paekche is often referred to as "the lost kingdom," since very few of its historical records and artifacts have survived. This single incense burner, however, is a rich source of information on the art, lifestyle, and thoughts of the ancient Paekche people. It is partly for this reason that the work has received so much attention, as its archaeological significance is great.

The Gilt-Bronze Incense Burner of Paekche (National Treasure No. 287) was cast in bronze and plated with gold, although much of the gold has disappeared with the passing of time. It is a remarkably large object, measuring 61.8cm in height, 19cm in diameter and weighing 11.85kg. It is the tallest known *boshanlu*-type censer in Asia, although this is not the only aspect that distinguishes the Paekche incense burner from other such artifacts. Its true significance lies in the dynamic and diverse cultural symbolism captured with the inspired beauty of its body and design.

The burner has three sections: the main body, the pedestal stand, and the lid. The incense bowl is in the form of a lotus flower, and is supported by a stand in the shape of a dragon. The domed lid of the bowl represents the mythological Taoist mountain, with many layered peaks. At the very top of the lid is a phoenix, its wings spread wide and its tail quivering in the wind, as if it had just landed gently on the immortal hills. Incense was put in the bowl and the fragrant smoke passed through the holes in the lid.

On the incense burner, there are in total 74 mountain peaks, dozens of human figures, and almost 100 animals, all of which are portrayed with realism. The figures who appear on the incense burner inform us of the daily life of the ancient Paekche people. Directly below the phoenix at the top are five musicians, each playing a different musical instrument. Both the instruments and facial expressions are depicted in detail.

Between the mountains and valleys, we find people engaged in various activities. One man sits peacefully immersed in meditation, while another washes his long hair in front of a waterfall. Another man is seen taking a walk along a mountain path with his dog. Another sits on top of a rock leisurely

Gilt-Bronze Incense Burner of Paekche

6th century AD, H 61.8cm, National Treasure No. 287, Puyo National Museum

fishing in a pond, making gentle ripples.

On and in between the petals of the lotus flower, we find fish, deer, cranes and dancing figures. These appear in perfect balance with their counterparts in the hills. This creative technique of related motifs linked the upper and lower parts of the censer in a harmonious unity.

There is hardly any space on the surface of the incense burner which is not filled. Various decorative motifs such as hills, streams, rocks, human figures, as well as animals in motion like fish and birds, some real others imaginary, are included to give life to the elliptical sphere of the body. This vitality is affirmed by the pedestal stand, which is in the image of a spirited yet playful dragon about to ascend to the sky. Three of its legs are arranged to form a circle, creating a stable base, while its fourth foot is raised in the air. If all four feet were on the ground, the visual equilibrium of the incense burner would have been compromised. The dragon is depicted in detail, yet nothing is superfluous. It is full of energy, yet it is perfectly balanced.

In this incense burner, we can discern the Taoist and Buddhist beliefs that were widespread in the ancient kingdoms of Korea. The mountain inhabited by the phoenix, immortals, and imaginary plants and animals is based on the cosmology of Taoism, while the lotus petals which appear throughout the main body of the incense burner reflect the influence of Buddhism, and the belief that everyone in the Pure Land of Buddha is born from a lotus flower. The censer is also a portrayal of the ideal world in which the people of Paekche wanted to live. It is a peaceful world in which people, animals and nature coexist happily with one another.

The Gilt-Bronze Incense Burner of Paekche is a fine work of art, the making of which required many different techniques including the three-dimensional phoenix, the various carved motifs and the high-spirited dragon. No other censers of this period can be compared with this incense burner, either in terms of artistic or technical accomplishment. Moreover, as it is a harmonious integration of nature and humankind, Taoism and Buddhism, real world and ideal world, it is widely acclaimed to be the most profound and symbolic incense burner ever produced in the Far East.

14. Pensive Bodhisattva

There are two pensive Bodhisattva statues, designated as National Treasures No. 78 and No. 83 in Korea, which are considered by many art historians to be among the finest examples of ancient Korean art. In both statues, the Bodhisattva is represented sitting in deep meditation, with the right leg resting on the left thigh, and fingers held up close to the right cheek. This is based on an event in the life of Shakyamuni Buddha before he attained enlightenment, while he was still a prince. As he was watching farmers at work in the fields one day, he saw birds swooping down to catch insects which had been disturbed by the plough, and became aware of the sufferings of sentient beings. In Korea, this seated image of a bodhisattva in the lotus-position traditionally represented the Maitreya Bodhisattva, or Buddha of the future, because of the influence of the Maitreya cult that was prevalent in East Asia.

Though the image of the pensive Bodhisattva originated in India, and passed through Central Asia and China before it reached Korea, it was in the hands of the ancient Korean sculptors in the early 7th century that it achieved its most beautiful form. The pensive Bodhisattva statues of the Three Kingdom period in Korea (Koguryo, Paekche and Silla) are agreed to be perfect examples of their kind, and for this reason Japanese scholars have often referred to the pensive sitting position when it appears in statues as "the image of the Three Kingdoms."

The true virtue of this statue is that it reveals through its simple but graceful form the noble mindset of the pensive Bodhisattva, without the need for

Pensive Bodhisattva
Early 7th century AD,
Gilt-bronze, H 93.5cm,
National Treasure No. 83,
Seoul National Museum

complexity or excessive use of decoration. Those who behold the statue find themselves purified by the serenity which overflows from calm silence. Gazing upon its inner self, with a peaceful smile illuminating its whole expression, the statue conveys the bliss of enlightenment experienced in an egoless mental state.

Left: Gilt-Bronze Pensive Bodhisattva at Seoul National Museum, Korea

Right: Wooden Pensive Bodhisattva at Koryu-ji Temple, Japan

At Koryu-ji temple in Kyoto, Japan, there is a Maitreya Bodhisattva statue which is greatly treasured by the Japanese. This wooden statue is almost identical to Korean National Treasure No. 83, not only in respect of the figure's position, but also in the shape of the head, the folds of the clothes, and the waist belt which hangs to one side of the stool.

The only difference is in the material; one is made with gilt-bronze and the other is made of wood. These different materials mean that the statues differ slightly in ambience. Studies by Korean and Japanese scholars, as well as the American art historians Jon Carter Covell and Evelyn McCune, have established that the statue at Koryu-ji was made in Korea and transported to Japan in the early 7th century.

In both cases, the slenderness of the statue's upper body renders an appearance that is neither sensual nor earthly. All attention is drawn to the face, downcast eyes, and delicate fingers gently touching the cheek. With their simple yet refined manner, the statues perfectly express the noble spirit of the Bodhisattva, meditating on the sufferings of human beings, and how to ease their suffering.

The Koryu-ji Bodhisattva was originally covered with gold, but as time passed this all but disappeared. The aesthetics of the statue are in a sense heightened by the soft texture of the wood beneath. Karl Jaspers (1883~1969), the German philosopher, discovered this statue in the course of his studies in world art history and remarked:

> In the Maitreya Bodhisattva of Koryu-ji Monastery we behold a perfect and natural expression of the supreme ideals of truly perfect existence. I believe this is a symbol of the purest, most harmonious, all-enduring attitude of the human soul, which surpasses the temporal limitations of worldly affairs. During the several decades of my life as a philosopher, I have never seen a work of art so expressive of the real tranquility of human existence. This Buddhist sculpture symbolizes in its plainest form the ultimate ideal of permanent peace and harmony, to which every human heart aspires.
>
> – Karl Jaspers, "Beyond the Defeat of War"

Undoubtedly, the pensive Bodhisattva statues are supreme examples of religious art. With their pure and profound spiritual beauty, they reach out to the hearts of those who see them, transcending time, space and belief.

15. The Sacred Bell of King Songdok

The Sacred Bell of King Songdok (National Treasure No. 29) received the following words of praise from the Japanese art critic Yanagi Muneyoshi (1889~1961): "In terms of sheer beauty, it is without equal in the East." Dr. Otto Kümmel (1874~1952), director of East Asian Arts at the National Museum of Germany, once visited the museum in Kyongju where the bell is now kept, and remarked that the museum's description of the bell as "the best in Korea" should be altered to "the best in the world." He further remarked that in Germany, this single bell would have an entire museum devoted to it.[1]

The Sacred Bell was originally used in a temple to mark times of prayer or general assembly. Together with these practical functions, the pure and graceful ringing of a temple bell was thought to represent the Buddha's voice, and so calm the mental sufferings of sentient beings. The Sacred Bell was commissioned by King Kyongdok, the 35th ruler of Silla, out of devotion to his father King Songdok. 27 tons of bronze were used in the making of the bell. The King died before the task was finished, and his son King Hyegong completed the bell in AD 771 in deference to his father's wishes.

It is the largest bell of its kind surviving in Korea today, standing 3.75m high and weighing 18.9 tons (approximately equal to 12 mid-sized cars). The casting techniques of the Silla people who created this enormous and beautiful bell 1200 years ago are still not fully understood. Modern engineers can make bells of a

---

[1] Kwak Dong-hai, *Temple Bell: The Sound of Life*, p. 97.

similar size without much difficulty, but only with the help of blast furnaces and other modern equipment. Within the technological limitations of Silla period, however, it would be hard for today's experts to manufacture such a bell.

A surprising feature of this 18.9 ton bell is that it can be suspended from a horizontal iron rod with a diameter of 8.5cm. In 1975, when the bell was moved from its previous site to the National Museum in Kyongju, an attempt was made to replace this old rod with a new one. This turned out to be difficult, as the ring through which the rod had to be inserted was only 9cm in diameter. According to modern theories of engineering, the rod would need to be at least 15cm in diameter in order to be able to withstand the weight. Analysis revealed that the original rod was created by hammering many thin layers of alloyed metals into a solid cylindrical mass, making it unnaturally strong. The original rod was therefore retained, and is still in use today.

The ring at the top of the bell is dragon-shaped. The rod is inserted beneath the dragon's belly, and attached to the belfry.

For art lovers, the most attractive features of the bell are the depictions of heavenly beings which appear on the main body. The angels reverently hold incense burners in their hands as if to offer them up to the Buddha, quietly scenting their surroundings. The long and delicate lines of leaves and tendrils, which twine around each angel and waft heavenwards, add a lively mystique to the beauty of the bell. The floral objects floating in the air could be seen as heavenly clouds, or could be interpreted as the deep reverence of the heavenly beings towards Buddha, which is transformed into flames and smoke as the reverence reaches out to the heavens.

The beauty of its visual design is only one aspect of the bell's splendor. The true essence of any bell is the sound that it creates. The Sacred Bell emits a majestic and graceful sound, with a subtle yet persistent resonance that leaves a lasting impression on the heart of the listener. Tsuboi Ryohei, a Japanese scholar who specializes in the study of bronze bells, compared the musical quality of bronze bells from different countries in a documentary produced for the Japanese television station NHK. He concluded that the Divine Bell of King Songdok was by far the most developed and sonorous.

The reason for the Sacred Bell's deep, resonant notes, which penetrate the mind of the listener, lies in the unique structure of Korean bells. The sound of a bell must be clear and loud, but it must also reverberate, alternating between loud and soft, and the ringing should continue for a long time even if it is struck only once. In physics, this effect is called the "beat phenomenon" as the sound pulsates like a heart beat. This beat effect, whereby the sound continues to be revived even though it appears to be dying out, is a distinctive feature of Korean bells.

The reason for this beat phenomenon is the intentional asymmetry of the bell's design. Bells with varying levels of wall thickness always create two sound waves with differing frequencies. The difference in frequency leads to the beat phenomenon. It does not occur in Western bells, as these are generally of a consistent thickness.

On the top of the Sacred Bell there is a "sound pipe," 96cm in length. These pipes are found exclusively in Korean bells, and their function was unknown until very recently. Professor Um Young-ha of Seoul National University concluded through experiments with different models of bell that the sound pipe serves as an "acoustic filter".

When the bell is struck, sound waves are produced both inside and outside the bell. Inside the bell, the various tones collide and interfere with one another due to the confined space, and the noise created by this interference affects the overall sound of the bell. The pipe was added to the top of bell in order to improve the sound quality by providing a release for these conflicting sound waves.

The quality of the bell's sound is enhanced even further by a hollow dug in the ground underneath the bell. Western bells are frequently kept in towers, and rung by means of a clapper hanging inside the bell. Korean bells are usually suspended only a short distance from the ground, with the depression in the earth beneath them serving as an amplifier. On a clear night, the Sacred Bell is said to have been heard over a distance of forty miles.

Even after 1200 years, the exquisite beauty and scientific genius of King Songdok's Sacred Bell cannot be fully understood. Consisting of 1,037 ancient Chinese characters, the inscription on the body of this extraordinary bell begins as follows:

Profound truth encompasses invisible phenomena. Thus, even though one looks, one cannot see it. Even though its thunder fills the space between Heaven and Earth, one cannot know the source. For this reason, the Buddha taught the truth using parables, according to the time and the listener. Likewise, the sacred bell was made so that sentient beings might hear the perfect sound of truth.

Sacred Bell of King Songdok

771 AD, H 365.8cm, National Treasure No. 29, Kyongju National Museum

16. Sokkuram Grotto

Mount Toham, the first point in the historic city of Kyongju to meet the sunrise, is a sacred mountain that has always been revered by the people of Silla. Near the bottom of the mountain is the Pulguksa temple, one of the most beautiful shrines in Korea. Here can be found many cultural sites that appear in Kyongju guidebooks, such as the Blue and White Cloud Bridge stone staircases, and the Shakyamuni and Great Treasure pagodas.

From the gate of Pulguksa temple, if you follow the winding mountain path through a nearby forest for about an hour, you will find a small wooden building on a mountain slope. The building is 565 meters above sea level, and from it one can make out the distant blue waves of the East Sea. Sheltered inside is the Sokkuram Grotto, a 1200 year old mystery of architectural design. According to the *Memorabilia of the Three Kingdoms* (1281), the Pulguksa Temple and the Sokkuram Grotto were completed over the course of three decades under the direction of Prime Minister Kim Tae-song, when Silla was at the height of its prosperity during the middle of the eighth century AD.

Throughout its long history, Korea has produced many beautiful and extraordinary works of art. Of all these, the Sokkuram Grotto might be considered the finest. It is a sublime achievement, embodying the perfect and ideal harmony of science, art and religion in a single entity. Scholars across the world have praised the Sokkuram Grotto, calling it "an eternal masterpiece" (Yanagi Muneyoshi), "the Parthenon of the East" (Jon Carter Covell), and "the most exemplary classical work of the Orient" (Andre Eckardt).

The World's Only Man-Made Grotto

Cave temples originated from the *Chaitya* of India, the birthplace of Buddhism. The people of India built *stupas* and held religious services inside the caves to escape the hot climate. This tradition passed over to Central Asia and China, eventually reaching Korea.

Though inspired by the cave temples of India and China, Sokkuram fundamentally differs from them in its construction. The cave temples were built by digging into hillsides and carving on naturally-occurring rocks. However, the surfaces of Korea's hills and mountains often consist of solid granite, which made it impossible to build temples similar to those of Karle or Ajanta, who created thousands of *stupas* and statues in areas with softer mixtures of rock and clay.

In order to construct the Sokkuram Grotto, the people of Silla had to develop new building techniques. They used more than 360 large blocks of granite to build an unprecedented artificial cave, which consisted of a rectangular antechamber, a main hall with a domed ceiling, and a corridor connecting the two structures. The Sokkuram Grotto is therefore unlike the natural grottos found in other countries, and is in fact the only man-made example of its kind. It is also more than just a simple arrangement of sculptures. It is a construction of great thought and precision.

With the main statue of Buddha at the center, the grotto originally contained a total of 40 Buddhist sculptures[2], including Bodhisattvas, the Ten Disciples of

---

[2] Only 38 of these sculptures remain, two having been stolen during the Japanese occupation of Korea.

Main Hall of the Sokkuram Grotto

8th century AD, National Treasure No. 24, Mt. Toham, Kyongju

the Buddha, Four Heavenly Kings and the guardian Devas. All the sculptures were created with such artistic skill that the hard granite surfaces of each one seem almost alive.

The most impressive feature of the Sokkuram Grotto is the main Buddha statue. It is particularly special because it represents the most sacred event in the life of the Buddha, the moment when he achieved enlightenment. In this statue, we see the spiritual seeker Shakyamuni attaining Buddhahood, as he reaches his great awakening under the Bodhi tree at Bodhgaya. For many years, the original statue which captured this sacred moment was kept in the Mahabodhi Temple of Bodhgaya, but it has since disappeared.

According to *Ta Tang Hsi Yu Chi* (629), an account of the Chinese Buddhist Master Hsuan-tsang's pilgrimage to India along the Silk Road, the original Buddha statue at the Mahabodhi Temple had a sitting height of 3.36m, a width of 1.88m across the shoulders, and a width of 2.69m between the knees. The statue showed the Buddha facing east and touching the ground with his fingers (*dhyna-mudra*), symbolizing his final overcoming of all the attempts of demons to break his resolution to become a Buddha, and his calling to Earth to witness the moment. Astonishingly, the Buddha statue of Sokkuram conforms to the exact dimensions, orientation and hand gestures of the original Bodhgaya statue, whose appearance is now only preserved in historical records. Since no other Buddhist statue recreates the moment of enlightenment with such faithfulness, the main Buddha statue of Sokkuram Grotto is regarded as the archetype of all Buddha statues.[3]

The Beauty of Holiness

Since ancient times, marble and granite have been the most common materials used for stone sculpting. Marble is relatively easy to use as its texture is fine and soft. It can be used to represent delicate items such as rose petals or the minute creases in clothing. On the other hand, granite is very difficult to use for detailed objects because it is hard and coarse-grained. It is therefore more

---

[3] The iconographic origin of the statue remained unknown until the Korean art historian Kang Woo-bang discovered it in Hsuan-tsang's records and analyzed the religious symbolism in 1987 (*Misul Charyo* Vol. 38).

Main Buddha statue at Sokkuram

(H 3.36m, Granite) recreating the moment of Buddha's enlightenment

suitable for simple or abstract images rather than subtle and detailed ones.

Despite this, the granite sculptures of Sokkuram are extremely detailed and realistic. It is as if each of the sculptures, in their free postures, is ready to step out of the wall. The main Buddha statue was created with perfect dimensions and the highest artistic skill. The guardian statues express bravery and resolution, and the Four Heavenly Kings dignity and firmness. The Bodhisattvas possess their own gentle grace, and each Arhat exhibits its own unique characteristics. All the figures in the Sokkuram Grotto are considered to be among the greatest masterpieces in the history of East Asian Buddhist sculpting.

In the other cave temples of Asia, the walls and statues are often decorated with extravagant colors that dazzle the eye. However, the architects and the sculptors of the Sokkuram Grotto exercised restraint in the use of color, thereby creating a plain and holy ambience that calms the mind. Rather than eliciting exclamations of surprise from visitors, it evokes only a reverent silence.

The main statue of Buddha, who sits in the grand lotus seat, takes minimalism to its extreme. The number of lines in the robe can almost be counted, and there is no outward exaggeration or complexity in the statue's appearance. This very simplicity shows us an aspect of the enlightened Buddha, freed from all worldly attachments. It is the manifestation of the inner realm of spirituality that cannot be explained or evaluated. In the words of an art historian, "Those who have not seen it cannot talk about it, because they have not seen it, and those who have seen it cannot talk about it, because they *have* seen it."

In the very heart of the grotto there is a statue of the eleven-headed Bodhisattva Kuanum (Avalokiteshvara), who stands towards the back of the hall, gazing at the main statue of the Buddha. It is an exquisite sculpture that brings to mind the words of the Dutch scholar Gerardus van der Leeuw, "Beauty will guide us to holiness."

As the incarnation of compassion, Bodhisattva Kuanum is the most important of the Bodhisattvas. The eleven heads are symbolic of her deep love for mankind, as she constantly looks upon all sentient beings in need of her help (it was believed that one head would not be enough for such an immense task). This graceful statue of the Bodhisattva is located directly behind the main Buddha-statue, illustrating the Buddha's teachings and character with feminine virtue and beauty.

The more elaborate techniques of Silla artisans, used sparingly in the serene and profound image of Buddha attaining enlightenment, were freely employed in the statue of the Bodhisattva. The Bodhisattva gently holds prayer beads in her right hand. With her left hand, she holds a vase full of sweet nectar, in which a lotus flower — the symbol of Buddhism — is blossoming.

The whole statue basks in the majestic grandeur of sacred robes and bead jewelry. Such refined and graceful engraving techniques cannot be seen in any other Buddhist statues. The German scholar Andre Eckardt called it "an excellent statue, which could not well be exchanged for a hundred others."

Eleven-headed Kuanum Bodhisattva
H 2.44m, Granite

Union of Religion, Science and Art

When Shakyamuni Buddha became fully enlightened, he is said to have attained the realization that all things arise and perish according to causes and conditions. This means that no one being can exist independently of others, but everything that exists is dependent upon and related to another. A single tree cannot come into existence by itself. It is nourished by sunshine, rain and the soil at every stage of its life. Therefore a being is part of the universe, and the entire universe exists in the same being.

This principle (often referred to as "dependent origination"), which illustrates the organic and harmonious relationship between the part and the whole, is expressed in the Sokkuram Grotto by means of geometrical proportion. The main rotunda symbolizes the heavens or the realm of Truth, while the rectangular antechamber represents the earth or the realm of worldly existence, and both are contained within one large circle (see diagram in the following page). This symbolism expresses the Buddhist philosophy that Truth and worldly life are ultimately part of the same realm.

The diameter of the main hall, which measures 24 *tangchok* (7.2m), served as the basic unit of measurement, which determined the dimensions of every defined space within the grotto. 48 *tangchok* (14.4m), or twice the 24 *tangchok*, was the total length of the antechamber and the rotunda, while 12 *tangchok* (3.6m), or half the 24 *tangchok*, corresponds to the diameter of the Buddha's seat, as well as the width of the corridor connecting the antechamber and the rotunda. Consequently, the ground plan of the Sokkuram consists of inscribed or circumscribed circles with diameters of 12, 24 or 48 *tangchok*. The same geometrical patterns apply vertically as well as horizontally.

In his book *Thinking of Korea*, the Japanese art critic Yanagi Muneyoshi described the aesthetic and spiritual beauty of the organic unity of the grotto's

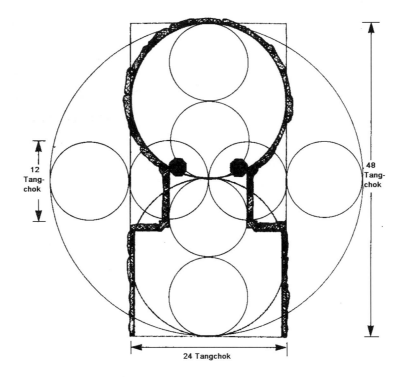

12
Tang-
chok

48
Tang-
chok

24 Tangchok

Ground plan (above) and side view (below) of the Sokkuram Grotto

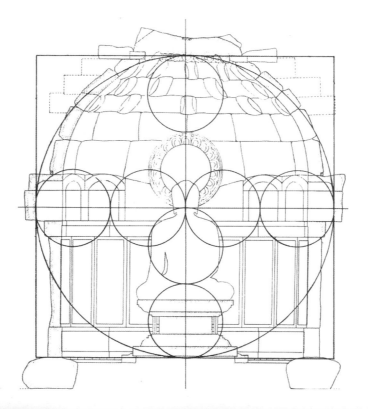

structure as follows:

> Sokkuram truly expresses the unified plan of a single mind. Unlike India's Ajanta caves or China's Longmen Grotto, the cave is not an assembly of sculptures accumulated over time. Throughout this tranquil creation, we see the workings of a single mind. It is an indivisible, organic whole in which none of the parts detracts from another. In both external and psychological terms, it is a complete unity of amazing thoroughness and detail. The unified structure gives an impression that the whole architecture is actually a single sculpture.

The beauty of such symmetry and the sense of spiritual unity are based on highly accurate mathematical calculations and ingenious building techniques. Dr. Nam Chun-woo, former professor of physics at Seoul National University, claimed that "As we research the grotto's structure, we would become more and more aware of its extraordinary mathematical harmony." In the May 1969 issue of *Shindonga* magazine, Dr. Nam further explained the wonders of Sokkuram's construction as follows:

> The Sokkuram Grotto was constructed with a phenomenal level of geometrical accuracy. The margin of error was only 1 in 10,000. When we consider that an accuracy of 1 in 10,000 means a discrepancy of 1 millimeter in every 10 meters, we get a sense of how accurately each of the grotto's stones was placed…One cannot help but be amazed at the way the Silla people sculpted large blocks of granite as if they were working with pieces of dough, or their knowledge of geometry that formed the basis of such an

undertaking…They must have correctly calculated the value of the circular constant [π] far in excess of 7 decimal places, and it is likely at the very least that they had the geometric knowledge to apply the sine law to a regular dodecahedron, namely to calculate the precise value of the sine function of 9°.

The intricate architecture of the Sokkuram Grotto is nowhere more evident than in the design of the domed ceiling, which is made up of 108 stones each weighing tens of tons. The wall of the dome comprises five rows of granite panels, with a round stone at the top in the shape of a lotus flower. From the third row to the fifth row, a total of 30 supporting stones were placed in between the panels, protruding on the outside and holding the panels on either side in place (see picture on the following page). Unlike the lower two rows, which are almost vertical, the angle of slope becomes very steep from the third row upwards, and these supporting stones served to prevent the structure from collapsing inwards, just as an ornamental hairpin is inserted to hold an arrangement in a woman's hair.

Thanks to these stone rivets, known as *tongtuldol* in Korean, the dome remains in perfect equilibrium. It is able to support the weight of the enormous stones without the use of any adhesive agent. If a single stone were to be removed, however, the dome's huge stone panels would lose tension and immediately collapse. In other words, each and every one of the stones, which together number more than 100, depends on another for support. Here, the organic unity of the part and the whole is affirmed once again.

In conclusion, the Sokkuram Grotto may be regarded as a true masterpiece, which artistically and architecturally recreates the most important event in the life of Shakyamuni Buddha – the moment of enlightenment – and also his greatest realization – the principle of dependent origination. There are many

A sectional image of the Sokkuram Grotto displayed in the Silla Museum of Arts and Science in Kyongju. The stone rivets provide perfect structural balance, and as a result the domed ceiling can support the weight of the enormous stone panels without the use of an adhesive agent.

other grottos and Buddha statues in China and India that are larger than Sokkuram, but none were created with such detailed, systematic and geometrical planning, or with such flawless, timeless beauty. In these respects, Sokkuram is a unique Buddhist heritage, the like of which cannot be found anywhere in the world.

Even after 1200 years, the profound spiritual beauty and religious atmosphere of the Sokkuram, with its blend of sublime art and scientific precision, invites today's viewers to inner reflection and meditation.

17. Koryo Celadon: Creating Jade with Clay

Koryo celadon pottery occupies a special place among the world-class cultural assets of Korea, and in the history of world ceramics. It is a unique form of art, which has been admired and appreciated by art lovers of East and West alike. When the famous British potter Bernard Leach (1887~1979) first saw the subtle bluish-green color of Koryo celadon, it is said that he was deeply impressed and exclaimed, "How many people could I make happy, if I could reproduce this color myself!" Another renowned ceramic specialist William Honey stated in his book, *The Ceramic Art of China and Other Countries of the Far East* (1945) "The best Korean wares are not only original; they are the most gracious and unaffected pottery ever made. They have every virtue that pottery can have."

Even the Chinese, who possess the world's richest tradition in ceramics, have shown a high regard for Koryo celadon. Taiping Laoren of Song China wrote about the world's greatest treasures in his book *Xiu Zhong Jin*, and stated that the jade color of Koryo celadon is the "best of its kind under the heavens." In a famous account of his journey to Korea in 1123, the Chinese civil official Xu Jing, who was a contemporary of Taiping Laoren, praised Koryo celadon in similar terms, commenting on its "exquisite color and form".

Koryo celadon's gently flowing curves and delicate bluish-green glaze refresh the eyes and the mind of the viewer. The semi-transparent glaze, reminiscent of a clear sky after a storm, is the essence of the Koryo celadon's beauty. The color is so subtle and delicate that it appears to be a feature of the clay itself, rather than something artificially applied.

Celadon is created with clay and glaze that contain a small amount of iron. When the pottery is fired in a kiln, the iron oxidizes and produces the unique jade color of Koryo celadon. The temperature inside the kiln is kept between 1250°C and 1300°C. This high temperature must be maintained for 24 hours in order to achieve the coloring effect. Considering that this work was being done a millennium ago, we can infer that the Koryo potters not only possessed advanced tools and equipment, but were also very experienced in temperature control.

However, technology alone cannot explain or create the beauty of Koryo celadon. Even today, when the clay, glaze and other materials used to make the celadon have been chemically analyzed, and the process of firing pottery at high temperatures has become so much easier, modern potters have failed to replicate the true mystical beauty of celadon. Creating high quality celadon appears to have required a spiritual devotion on the part of the Koryo potters. They believed that in order to create truly perfect celadon pottery, three things must be true. First, the country must be at peace and the people content with their lives. Second, the potter must have a pure mind and be of the highest skill. Third, the country must be united as one. If all these circumstances were in place, the celadon would display a unique, subtle and enchanting beauty.

Koryo celadon craftsmanship reached its zenith in the period between the 12th and early 13th century. During these years, celadon had many different uses. Examples of typical celadon wares include tea cups, wine bottles, incense burners, flower vases, perfume containers, brush holders, water droppers (used in calligraphy and painting) and even pillows and roof tiles. They were also made

Facing Page: Above. Ribbed bottle (Left), Water dropper in the shape of peach (Right)
Below. Incense Burner with openwork design (Left), Ewer with peony design (Right)

Celadon Ewer 13th century, H 32.7cm, Samsung Museum of Art

in a variety of forms inspired by nature, such as lotus flowers, bamboo, peaches, pomegranates, gourds and also animals and birds including ducks, turtles, dragons, lions and monkeys.

Around 1200 AD, *chinsa* celadon first appeared. The *chinsa* color was achieved using copper oxide. A picture or design was painted on the surface of celadon ware using *chinsa*, and the glaze was then applied. When the celadon was heated at a high temperature, the oxidized copper turned an attractive deep red color, making a beautiful contrast with the jade-green background.

Very few works of *chinsa* celadon have survived. Of those that remain, the ewer shown on the previous page is one of the finest examples. Made in the shape of a gourd, it has a gently curving handle and spout, which reflect the elegant tastes of the Koryo period.

The body and lid are carved to represent a lotus blossom, with a small lotus flower above and a larger one below. The veins of each petal have been carved delicately with cinnabar-red outlines. White dots like dew drops are added occasionally to enhance the impression of purity and serenity. At the neck of the ewer there is a child monk bearing a lotus bud, and a tiny frog is poised on top of the handle, as if it has just jumped out of a pond.

An eminent example of underglazed red-copper ornament, used for the first time in the world during the Koryo period, this ewer demonstrates the skill and accomplishment of the Koryo potters. The achievement would not have been possible without advanced smelting techniques, since an understanding of the different melting points of metals is required to produce the refined red copper glaze. In addition to its technical artistry, this rare and beautiful ewer is testament to the rich imagination and deep love of nature possessed by the Koryo potters.

Since antiquity, jade has been considered the most auspicious gemstone, and in East Asia continuous attempts were made over the centuries to recreate its mystical appearance artificially. The Chinese potters eventually succeeded in creating a form of celadon with a color very close to that of jade. They called it *pi-saek* ('secret color'), as it could only be found in palaces, due to the reverence in which it was held. Yet it was not a wholly satisfactory reproduction of the jade color, and when the Koryo potters made their own version of celadon, the Chinese gave it the name of *pi-saek* also. In this case the 'pi' meant 'jade', thus acknowledging that Koryo celadon was the truest jade color.

The Koryo potters who had succeeded in making jade out of clay wanted to add patterns to the serene bluish-green surface. By training their hands endlessly and focusing their minds tirelessly, they finally succeeded in achieving this goal. With the so-called *sanggam* inlay, Koryo potters took jade celadon to another level of sophistication, and opened a new chapter in the history of world ceramics.

Sanggam was inspired by the inlay technique, whereby designs are engraved on the surface of metals and filled with another material such as gold and silver. Koryo potters applied this technique to celadon. Using bamboo knives, they cut out patterns in clay vessels which had been half-dried, often depicting scenes from nature. These designs on the clay wall were filled with white and red clay, and the vessels were fired. During this process, the red clay became black, and the white clay remained white. A translucent glaze was then applied and the vessels were fired again.

It is difficult to make celadon pottery without cracking occurring during the firing process, even when using only one type of clay. The success of *sanggam* inlay, which involved the use of different clays, was therefore a remarkable feat. For potters to achieve the *sanggam* effect, they needed to have an accurate understanding of the differing properties of clay and the appropriate temperatures at which to heat them. As a result, neighboring countries abandoned their attempts to make inlaid patterns in celadon, and simply applied paint directly to the pottery. The Koryo potters, however, persisted in their attempts and finally succeeded in mastering the *sanggam* technique, thereby making a valuable contribution to the richness of ceramic art.

The best of Koryo inlaid celadon is truly breathtaking, with its vibrant designs, clean and even forms, and the subtle yet alluring combinations of white, black and green. The famous celadon plum vase with inlaid cranes and clouds,

Celadon Plum Vase Inlaid with Crane and Cloud Designs

12-13th Century, H 42cm, National Treasure No. 68, Kansong Art Museum

now housed at Kansong Art Museum in Seoul, exhibits the *sanggam* inlay technique at the height of its development. Choi Soon-woo, a former director of the National Museum of Korea, compared its beauty to masterpieces of silk embroidery:

No matter how exquisite or lavish the silk embroideries may be, there are probably none that can compare with the dignified beauty and elegance of this *sanggam* inlay celadon. The design appears complicated and yet simple. Its quiet beauty and splendor are in harmony and subtly touch the viewer's heart…The clear blue glaze represents Koryo's sky, and the Koryo people knew very well how to fill this beautiful sky. They set carefree white clouds adrift in it, and between the white clouds, they offered their wishes to the heavens on the wings of a crane.[4]

Born from Korean clay and fire, and the devotion of Koryo potters, Koryo celadon is more than a cultural asset – it is a reflection of the Korean spirit and character. With a rich history of development behind its exquisite beauty, Koryo celadon has become a symbol of the culture of Korea, as well as a valuable addition to the world's ceramic heritage.

---

[4] Choi Soon-woo, *A Journey to Korean Beauty,* p.233.

18. Koryo Buddhist Paintings

Together with celadon pottery, the Buddhist paintings of the Koryo period (AD 918~1392) have gained an international reputation since they appeared in the middle ages. Tang Hou of Yuan China described Koryo Buddhist paintings as "delicate and highly elaborate" in his book *Critique of Paintings Past and Present*, and in Japan, they have received even greater acclaim as works of "divine artistry." Today, well-known museums in the West such as the Guimet Museum in Paris, the Museum of Berlin, and the Metropolitan Museum of Art also have examples of Koryo Buddhist paintings in their collections.

The same refined curves of Koryo celadon can be found in Koryo Buddhist paintings, and the painstaking labor of inlay techniques is echoed in the detailed decorative patterns. The most notable characteristic is the intricacy of the gold boundary lines, which contrast with the brilliant mineral colors of red, blue and green. These colors are themselves remarkable, as they have hardly faded in the past seven hundred years.

Koryo was a devoutly Buddhist country, and the beliefs and ideals of its people are clearly expressed in these works of art. Koryo Buddhist paintings were made in order to glorify the compassion and virtue of Buddha and Bodhisattvas, and also served to help people understand the Buddhist scriptures by illustrating them visually.

In modern day abstract paintings, "line, color and form" are the standards by which a painting is measured. Buddhist painters had the further aim of invoking

**Detail of
Water Moon
Kuanum**
14th century,
color on silk

religious awe and reverence in their viewers. Thus they devoted their souls, as well as their technical abilities, to endow the works with gravity, delicacy and grace. Their resolve would have required decades of training and a lifelong dedication.

Fifteen Thousand Buddhas in One Painting

There are few Asian Buddhist paintings of any age that are comparable to those of Koryo in terms of intricacy and "infinite labor." Let us examine the Vairocana Buddha (Buddha of Light), kept at the Hudoin temple in Japan.

At first glance, it looks like an ordinary painting, but upon closer inspection, the painting reveals its hidden qualities. The words "Fifteen Thousand Buddhas" are written at the top of the painting, which is 175cm tall and 80cm wide. The painting depicts a peaceful Buddha sitting alone, with a radiant aura surrounding his head and body. It is not at first obvious why the painting is entitled "Fifteen Thousand Buddhas" when only one Buddha is painted.

Detail of Fifteen Thousand Buddhas 14th century, color on silk

The painting can be divided into three parts: the background, the borders and the Vairocana Buddha himself. When the characters of the words "Fifteen Thousand Buddhas" are examined closely, one sees that they are completely filled with the tiny faces of Buddhas. When the Buddha's robe is magnified, it reveals that it too is made up of countless tiny faces of Buddhas. The background of the painting is packed with these small faces arranged in perfect lines, like the pixels of a computer screen. The size of each Buddha's face is about 5 millimeters (0.2 inches) and they are all painted in gold. They are the micro-dimension of this work, which cannot be seen from a distance.

Another Koryo Buddhist painting, housed at Kobe City Museum, contains 8,000 Buddhas on a canvas that is 1.96 meters tall by 1.33 meters wide. In the center of the canvas is a square section containing Buddha and a group of disciples. The rest of the canvas consists of many small Buddhas.

The 8,000 Buddhas are clothed in red robes and are surrounded by a green radiance. Each Buddha has a different facial expression, with some smiling, some meditating, some tilting their heads, some chanting and so on. Unlike Buddhas in other Asian paintings, in which the faces do not vary greatly, the expressions of the Buddhas in this painting are all diverse and lifelike.

Besides the skill necessary to create images on such a minute scale, the time and patience that would have been required is almost beyond belief. One cannot but wonder why the painters undertook such a difficult task, or the meaning of the tiny Buddhas that fill the canvas.

According to the *Hwaom Sutra*, when Vairocana Buddha attains enlightenment, he exudes a radiance that fills the entire universe, and Buddhas appear from every pore of his body. In other words, these works are the illustration of the moment when the Buddha's enlightenment transforms the universe into a magnificent and holy place through the radiance of Truth.

The Gracious Realm of the Buddha

To date, approximately 160 Koryo Buddhist paintings have been identified. Among these, 10 remain in Korea and 20 are in North America and in Europe. The remaining 130 paintings are in Japan. Amongst these, some were sold or sent as gifts, but a large number of them appear to have been taken by Japanese pirates in the declining years of the Koryo dynasty and the Imjin War (1592~1598). As a result, Koryo Buddhist Paintings are better appreciated outside of Korea, especially in Japan.

Chion-ji Temple, an 800 year old building in Kyoto, is home to several Koryo Buddhist paintings. Among them is a picture that is highly esteemed by the Japanese. It is a painting of five hundred *Arhats* (disciples of the Buddha who have attained enlightenment) set against a scenic background of mountains and water.

The tiny paintings are on a canvas two meters in length, with each *Arhat* standing about 1.5cm tall. From a distance, they appear as hills, valleys and mountaintops. When people notice the 500 *Arhats* hidden in the design, they cannot help but be amazed. During an interview with the Korean Broadcasting System, a main national TV station, Professor Gikudake of Kyushu Institute of Technology said, "There was no other country in East Asia that possessed the techniques to produce such detailed and delicate paintings. These existed only in Koryo."

The Buddha and two Bodhisattvas are located in the center, and *Arhats* engaged in various activities make up the background. There are Arhats who appear thin and long-haired after periods of deep meditation inside a cave. There are also younger *Arhats* in intense discussion. Some are bathing their feet in a cool stream, others cleaning their bowl or robes. Another group of *Arhats* are preparing clothes and sutras for a retreat.

According to Buddhist scriptures, the Buddha appears as Bodhisattvas (Buddhist saints) and *Arhats* (enlightened spiritual practitioners) in order to lead all sentient beings to salvation. Therefore the *Arhats*, who serve as a bridge between Buddha's realm and the material world, are expressed in many different human forms. Such familiar images have helped Buddhism become more approachable.

Water Moon Kuanum

The painting of Water Moon Kuanum (Bodhisattva of Compassion) exhibits an elegant and subtle beauty, appropriate to its poetic name. This was one of the most popular varieties of Koryo Buddhist painting, and the subject matter has its origin in *Hwaom Sutra*, one of the most important Buddhist scriptures. In the Sutra, a young spiritual seeker named Sudhana meets the Bodhisattva Kuanum while on his long journey to enlightenment. Bodhisattva Kuanum sits upon a stool of mysterious rock encrusted with diamonds. Under her feet, there is a stream filled with precious corals and lotus blossom. In the bottom left corner of the painting, small Sudhana is seen paying his respects, kneeling down and pressing his palms together.

In this exquisite work, the first to stand out is the beautiful array of colors. Usually, the condition of paint deteriorates over hundreds of years. However, in this 14th century work painted on silk, the color of the paint and its adhesiveness is relatively well maintained. The pigments used here consist of four different natural minerals: lead, mercury, copper and gold. Instead of using artificial paints, which lose their color over time, the Koryo painters chose paints made from naturally occurring minerals.

Another interesting feature of this work is that the back of the canvas was

Water Moon Kuanum

Painted by Sokubag, 1323 AD, color on silk, H 165.5cm, W 101.5cm

painted as well the front. This is the secret of the vivid yet subtle colors of Koryo Buddhist paintings. On the front, only the outlines and the thin lines depicting the details are painted; most of the colors are painted on the back. In the eyes of the viewer, the colors therefore appear more subtle and subdued.

Just as Koryo celadon displays long and graceful curves, so do the lines of this painting. In particular, the lines of Buddha's robes are extremely smooth and detailed. No matter how long the line is, it remains constant in width. The gold-outlined edges weave in and out, or follow long curving lines that eventually end in folds with a pointed tip. The robes are almost comparable to the jewelry worn by the Bodhisattva in richness, their greatest quality being the transparency with which they are rendered. In this painting, however, the artist does not employ such lavish techniques excessively. They were used only to illustrate the Bodhisattva's clothes, thus emphasizing the sacredness of the Bodhisattva. In spite of the Bodhisattva's size, as the thin gold curves undulate in and out, there is a sense of lyricism and delicacy.

Bodhisattva Kuanum quietly radiates a light of serenity and compassion, with her head and body surrounded by a mysterious glow, like the moon rising in the night sky. The image has a religious significance, as the compassion of Bodhisattva Kuanum will give solace to anyone in need of it, just as the moon sheds its light on countless ponds and rivers. It is for this reason that the painting is entitled "Water Moon Kuanum."

19. Choson Ceramics

In Kyoto, the ancient capital city of Japan, there is a historic temple known as Daitoku-ji. The hermitage within this temple at Koho-an holds a tea bowl called "Kizaemon Yido." It is carefully stored in five layers of boxes, and is a highly treasured property of the temple. Several years ago, it was necessary for a visitor to pay 3,000 U.S. dollars to view the bowl just once. According to American art historian Jon Carter Covell, the abbot of Daitoku-ji once told her, "If the Koho-an hermitage should ever be destroyed by fire, and this single bowl were rescued and sold, there would be more than enough money to rebuild the entire temple."[5]

Rather surprisingly, this famous work of art was a very common variety of bowl, used by peasants in the south of Korea during the 15th and 16th centuries, known as *maksabal*. The name *maksabal* means a bowl (*sabal*) that was made by shaping the clay crudely (*mak*) before glazing and firing it. Since there was not much time and effort spent making the bowl, it is asymmetrical and the lines of its simple shape are irregular. Its design is not sophisticated, and its colors are far from lucid. However, when these simple ceramics, created without much effort or artistry, were taken to Japan and seen by the samurai and Zen monks, they were treated with a respect and honor that few other ceramic works received.

The Japanese art critic Yanagi Muneyoshi saw this bowl and was amazed by its humble beauty. He declared, "This common bowl, a worthless item that has

---

[5] Jon Carter Covell, *The World of Korean Ceramics*, p. 84.

become a precious treasure, demonstrates the true essence of beauty hidden in life." He further explained that its beauty comes from "truthfulness, naturalness and the absence of intention, extravagance and exaggeration." He then emphasized that other tea bowls cannot excel the *maksabal*, since they "self-consciously attempt to create beauty."[6]

The Korean potters of the Choson period (1392~1910) never produced highly decorated or colored work, and this resulted in what the Japanese considered "natural beauty (*wabi*)." Such aesthetic ideals, combined with the strong tea culture in Japan, meant that the unnoticed bowls of Korea, the work of anonymous potters, became precious works of art and a focus of admiration. During the Imjin War (1592~1598), the Japanese took hundreds of *maksabal* from the coastal areas of the Kyongsang province, which was located close to Japan. Among these, three are designated as Japanese national treasures and about twenty are designated as important cultural assets.

Japan's high regard for Korea's "common bowls" illustrates the status of Korean ceramic art in the world. Until the 17th century, only a few countries were able to produce works of porcelain. Korean potters, who were taken to Japan during the Imjin War, were responsible for the birth of Japanese porcelain in the 17th century. Even European countries, who lead the world's ceramic industry today, began to produce porcelain in the early 18th century.

In antique art auctions, Korean ceramics are often sold for the highest prices. In 1996, Christie's auction house sold a 17th-century Korean porcelain work for $8.41 million – twenty times its estimated value, causing a sensation in art markets worldwide.

---

[6] Yanegi Muneyoshi, *Thinking of Korea,* p. 310~321.

Punchong, Inspiration for Modern Ceramics

Bold. Earthy. Dynamic. Modern. These are some of the words associated with the *punchong* ware[1], a strikingly creative ceramic form produced during the first two hundred years of the Choson dynasty (1392~1910). The so-called "common bowls" that won much admiration from the Japanese were a type of *punchong* ware.

Due to the endless invasions of Mongols and Japanese pirates at the end of the Koryo dynasty (928~1392), the residents of the coastal regions were driven to inland areas. As a result, the major celadon kilns located near the coast, such as Kangjin and Puan, were abandoned, and the potters left their home towns and scattered all over the country. Celadon pottery, which was the dominant form in the ceramics of Koryo period, began to fade away with the decline of the Koryo dynasty

In the meantime, General Yi Song-gye established a new dynasty called Choson (1392~1910) and the potters who were scattered throughout the country came together to make celadons again. But the quality of celadon produced in this politically turbulent period could not match the refined beauty of the Koryo celadon. They were not the color of jade, but gray or yellowish. In such conditions, the *punchong* ware was born. It was typically covered either partially or wholly with the white slip used in *sanggam* inlaid celadons. Although the clay used in celadon and *punchong* wares was basically the same, *punchong* used the clay in a coarser form, with the white slip covering any defects.

Strangely, the difficult political situation gave potters considerable freedom to experiment with new styles. Because there were few established conventions during the transitional period, *punchong* wares are known for their varied and refreshing forms and patterns.

---

[1] *pun* = white slip (lit. "white powder"), *chong* = decoration

Left. ***Punchong* Jar**, 15~16th century, Samsung Museum of Art, Seoul
Right. ***Punchong* Bottle**, 15th century, Samsung Museum of Art, Seoul

Simple, freehand depictions of fish, birds, peonies, vines and other abstract geometrical designs often covered the greater portion of a vessel's surface, melting into its form and giving the impression of spontaneity. In decorative techniques, a variety of methods were developed by individual potters, who began with inlaid and stamped design and later moved on to other methods such as graffito, incised, iron-brown painting, brushed, fully immersed, and so on. In most cases white slip was used in the process.

The *punchong* wares are so innovative in spirit and expression that Bernard Leach, one of the most famous potters of the 20th century, once stated in a lecture he gave at Alfred University in the United States that the roadmap for modern ceramics had already been established by Korea's *punchong* wares, and that modern potters should plan their work accordingly. In his admiration for the "naked and unaffected freedom" of *punchong* wares, he later wrote as follows:

> These Korean pots grow like wildflowers. Their naïve abstractions and formalizations spring from quite another approach to living, a complete antithesis to our self-consciousness and calculations. The Koreans and their pots are childlike, spontaneous and trusting. We had something akin to this in Europe up to about the 13th century when religion and life were one, and the people who lived and worked in that modality were whole. It is the desire for wholeness which draws us to the Korean pots.

White Porcelain, In Pursuit of Serene Beauty

Together with *punchong* wares, white porcelain wares reached a unique level of beauty during the Choson period (1392~1910). White porcelain is created by applying translucent glaze to refined white clay, and firing it at temperatures between 1300~1350°C.

It is clear that plain white porcelain was more popular in Korea during this period than decorated porcelain. Because Choson was a state ruled by official-scholars who adhered strongly to the principles of Confucianism, they valued beauty which reflected serenity and elegance rather than extravagance and opulence. In a period when neighboring countries were producing ceramics with liberal use of color, Choson potters produced pure white ceramics, adding only minor decorations using cobalt blue or iron brown.

Bowl and Cover
White porcelain,
15th century, 22.7cm,
Horim Museum, Seoul

The ceramics of Choson Korea are not intended to amaze us with striking designs and techniques. Rather, they allow the viewers to feel happiness through their soft warmth and snow-like purity. This could be regarded as a truthful and innocent beauty that shows no greed or pride.

Although plain white-bodied porcelains made up the largest portion of Choson ceramics, decorated versions of the same wares were also produced in small numbers, especially towards the end of the dynasty. In blue-and-white colored wares, images of plum flowers, orchids, chrysanthemums and bamboo were the most favored. This group of four – known as the "Gentlemen Plants" – represented spring, summer, autumn, and winter, and were highly valued by the

Porcelain painted in underglaze cobalt blue

15th century, H 29.2cm, Horim Museum, Seoul

scholars as symbols of moral integrity. The plum flowers which blossom in the still cold weather of early spring, for example, were thought to represent the cultivation of noble spirit in face of adversity.

Porcelain painted in iron underglaze

17th century, H 53.8cm, Ewha University Museum, Seoul

Understandably, drawing on curved pottery is more difficult than drawing on a flat surface. It also requires a great deal of training to paint on porcelain, as its porous surface absorbs more water than paper or silk, and more brush movement is required. Besides, since iron brown glaze is more reactive to heat than cobalt blue, it is less easy to predict how the color will change during the firing process. Despite such difficulties, on the large white jar pictured above there is a lifelike painting of grapes and vines, which surpasses ink paintings on paper or silk in its elegance.

Grapes and vines in iron underglaze are confined to the upper section of the jar, leaving the lower part empty. The vine was painted diagonally across the jar's surface with darker colors, while light colors were applied to the leaves, and their outlines were painted in detail. Below the leaves are round grapes, again painted with darker colors. Normally, the designs on ceramics are purely decorative and cover the entire object. However, this painting of a grape vine is modest and restrained, leaving a more subtle and profound impression on the mind of the viewer. Without an equivalent in Chinese or Japanese ceramics, the so-called "moon jar" is regarded as the epitome of Korean white porcelain wares. With its attractive shape and generous proportions, the moon jar reflects the warm hearts of the Choson people, and their desire for a peaceful and fulfilling life.

It is impossible to make such a large round jar in a single piece, since the clay wall would initially be unable to support the weight of the upper section. Thus the large moon jars, measuring 40~50cm in height, were made by attaching two large bowls together. The middle of the jar shows a mark where the two bowls are joined together, and the overall shape is by no means symmetrical. Nevertheless, these flaws were accepted as part of the natural beauty of moon jars during the Choson period, and many people today are inclined to agree.

A magazine published by the British Museum relates a story that Bernard Leach, when browsing in a Seoul antiques store in the mid 1930s, came across a Choson dynasty moon jar and held his head in disbelief at its beauty. He bought the jar immediately, and walked out of the shop "carrying a piece of happiness." The jar now resides in the British Museum as one of the highlights of its Korean collection. In September 2007, the Museum held a special exhibition of traditional and modern Korean moon jars. It is one of several museums worldwide in which moon jars can be found.

Created in white without any decoration, the moon jar in its simplest form captivates the eyes and heart with its capacious and pleasing appearance, and the wholesomeness exuded by its pure color. Today moon jars are cherished by many of the world's art lovers for their plain and unadorned beauty.

Porcelain Moon Jar
18th century, H 42.5 cm, Private collection

20. The Garden of Changdok Palace

Since ancient times, Koreans have lived in natural surroundings that did not require great hardship or struggle. The country is surrounded by the sea on three sides, and instead of the extremes of bitter arctic cold and oppressive tropical heat, there are four distinct seasons. Water flowing into the valleys from the mountains is clear and clean enough to drink, and thanks to the soil and favorable weather, plants growing in the fields and mountains can often be used as medicinal herbs. As one medieval Arab historian observed, "There is seldom a stranger from another land who has traveled to this country and not settled there. The air is so wholesome, the water so pure and the soil so fertile – everything is found there in abundance."

Living in this blessed environment, Koreans came to realize and accept the rhythm of nature. They firmly believed that the ways of nature were intrinsically beautiful, and that it was wise to live and work in harmony with it.

Because nature was in their view something sacred and beautiful in itself, they adapted their gardens to nature, and not the other way round. Mountain features and streams, as well as boulders and trees, were preserved as far as possible in their natural state. They added only some resting places, and made some arrangements of trees and stones, but did not destroy or manipulate the natural order.

Houses were built and gardens cultivated in accordance with the landscape's natural characteristics, including its slopes and inclines. The land was never

made flat, and the buildings themselves were designed straight or curved, broad or narrow, depending on the existing topography. The garden of the Changdok Palace, one of the five great palaces of the Choson dynasty (1392~1910), is a fine illustration of this natural approach.

Following the completion of Kyongbok Palace in 1395 by King Taejo, the founder of the Choson dynasty, Changdok Palace was built in 1405 as a royal villa, or a secondary palace. Kyongbok was the principal palace, and was surrounded by the royal ancestral shrines and government offices. The capital city of Hanyang (present-day Seoul) was also built with the palace at center. However, the palace the monarchs preferred, and where they stayed the longest, was not Kyongbok, but Changdok. When the Choson dynasty ended in 1910, Changdok palace became government property and was opened to the general public. Even to this day, the beauty of the palace buildings and gardens has not faded.

The 74 acres of the gardens at Changdok consist of varied and often rolling landscape. The grounds contain 35 buildings, both large and small, and 7 artificial ponds, which together cover less than an acre. In other words, only 1% of the space is artificial or man-made. When UNESCO included Changdok Palace as part of the World Heritage in 1997, it described it as "an exceptional example of Far Eastern palace architecture and design, blending harmoniously with the surrounding landscape." It would be more correct to say that the Changdok garden is actually part of nature, rather than simply in harmony with it.

In traditional Korean gardens, there are no fountains, as it is natural for water to flow from higher place to a lower one. The stream lowers itself to become a river, and the river lowers itself even further until it cannot go any lower and reaches the sea. To Koreans, therefore, it was against the nature of water to make it shoot upwards to the sky. Instead, they made waterfalls. The ponds at Okryuchon, Puyongji and Aeryonji in the Changdok garden all had water sources positioned at a higher level so that water would fall downwards, like a miniature waterfall.

Another noteworthy feature of Royal Palace gardens in Korea is that deciduous trees are more commonly found than evergreen trees. In the case of China and Japan, evergreens were most often used, as they are insensitive to seasonal changes and so maintained a uniform beauty all year round. In the Korean mindset, the sprouting of new buds in spring and the fall of leaves in autumn represented the natural flow of the seasons, and to resist these seasonal changes did not lead to true beauty. Therefore, deciduous trees make up the majority of garden trees in Korea. A few pine trees and oriental arborvitae were also planted at intervals for variation. As a result, the gardens of Changdok feature a range of beautiful scenery unique to each season: springtime with the vitality of new life, summer with its leafy branches, fall with its reddening leaves, and winter tranquil with white snow.

Ponds, pavilions and flowerbeds, on the other hand, were intentionally designed with straight lines in order to make a contrast with nature. As the surrounding scenery was asymmetrical, if these structures were also given an irregular shape, it would create an impression of disorder. The straight-edged Puyongji pond, boundary walls erected with square-edged stones, the flowerbeds and chimneys with their simple geometric designs, all helped to create an atmosphere of order and peacefulness. Supplementing the beauty of nature with geometrical contrasts, whilst preserving their original beauty as far as possible, may be said to be the aesthetic goal and distinguishing feature of traditional Korean gardens.

In the gardens of western palaces, growth is cultivated along pathways in radial, circular or oblique lines. The beauty of such gardens is best appreciated from afar. The gardens of Changdok, however, were not intended only to be looked at. They were made as places of communion with nature. Thus it is only when we walk along the meandering paths, stretching out beneath hundred-year-old trees, noticing the small ponds, pavilions and waterfalls dotted between the hilltops and the woods that we can appreciate the true beauty of the garden. In these surroundings, the kings of the Choson dynasty would read books, take walks and compose poetry, sometimes in the companionship of courtiers, sometimes alone.

In this garden, full of reverence for nature and the virtue of humility, our bodies and minds feel free and comfortable, more so than in any luxurious garden. Here, the garden is not limited to stationary, contrived features such as walls and pavilions. The sky and clouds mirrored on the water, the murmuring of a stream along the valleys, and the breeze that touches leaves and flowers are all part of the whole, our companions sharing in the tranquil joys of nature.

Bibliography

Part 1 Print, Language & History

Boorstin, Daniel, *The Discoverers*, Random House, 1985.

Choi, Joon-sik, ed., *Twelve World Heritage in Korea*, Sigongsa, 2002.

Diamond, Jared, "Writing Right", *Discovery*, June 1994.

Jung, Soo-il, *World in Korea*, Changbi, 2005.

Kim, Dong-wook, *Suwon Hwasong Fortress*, Dolbegae, 2002.

Kim, Sung-soo, *Study of the Great Dharani Sutra of Undefiled Pure Radiance*, Cheongju Early Printing Museum, 2002.

Kim, Mun-shik, Shin, Byong-ju, *Uigwe*, Dolbegae, 2005.

Kim-Renaud, Young-Key, ed. *King Sejong the Great*, International Circle of Korean Linguistics, 1997.

Ledyard, Gari, *The Korean Language Reform of 1446*, University of California, Berkeley, 1966.

Man, John, *Alpha Beta: How 26 Letters Shaped the Western World*, Headline Book Publishing Ltd., 2001.

————, *The Gutenberg Revolution*, The Head line Review, 2003.

Park, Sang-jin, *The Secret of Tripitaka Koreana*, Gimm Young Publishers, 2007.

Sampson, Geoffrey, *Writing Systems: A Linguistic Introduction*, Tuttle Publishing, 1990.

Yang, Sung-jin, *Click into the Hermit Kingdom*, Dongbang Media, 2000.

Yi, Song-mu, *What is Choson Royal Sillok,* Dongbang Media, 2002.

Yi, Jong-ho, *Seven Wonders of Korea*, Wisdom House, 2007.

Part 2 Fine Art

Covell, Jon Carter, *Japan's Hidden History: Korean Impact on Japanese Culture*, Hollym, 1984.

————, *Korea's Colorful Heritage*, Si-sa-yong-o-sa Inc., 1985.

————, *The World of Korean Ceramics*, Si-sa-yong-o-sa, Inc., 1986.

————, Kim, Yu-kyong, trans, In Search of Korean Cultural Roots, Hakkojae, 1999.

Choi, Soon-woo, *A Journey to Korean Beauty*, Hakkojae, 2002.

Eckardt, Andre, Kwon, Yong-pil, trans., *A History of Korean Art*, Youlhwadang Publisher, 2003.

Han, Young-dae, Pak Kyung-hee, trans., *The Explorers of Korean Beauty*, Hakkojae, 1997.

Huh, Kyun, *Korean Garden: The World of Scholars*, Dareun Sesang, 2002.

Im, Doo-bin, *101 Masterpieces of Korean Art*, Garam, 1998.

Jang Soon-yong, *Changdok Palace*, Daewonsa, 1993.

Jung, Soo-il, *World in Korea*, Changbi, 2005.

Kang, So-yon, *Series of Articles on Korean Buddhist Paintings*, Hyudae Bulkyo, 2006~2007.

Kang, Woo-bang, *A Pilgrimage to Beauty*, Yekyong, 2001.

————, "La Porte d'Harmonie Applied to the Sokkuram Monument Proportion and Pratity-samutpada", *Misul Charyo*, Vol. 38, National Museum of Korea, 1987.

Kawk, Dong-hae, *Temple Bell: Sound of Life*, Hangil Art, 2006.

Moon, Myung-dae, *History of Korean Buddhist Art*, KPI Publishing Co., 1997.

Shin, Dae-hyun, *A Study on the Sarira Reliquary of Korea*, Hangil Art, 2003.

Shin, Yong-hoon, *Royal Palaces of Choson*, Chosun Ilbo, 1998.

Yanagi, Muneyoshi, Sim Woo-sung, trans., *Thinking of Korea*, Hakkojae, 1996.

Yoon, Yong-i, *Beautiful Ceramics of Korea*, Hakkojae, 1996.

Yu, Hong-june, *Smiles of the Baby Buddha*, Changbi Publishers, 1999.

Various authors, *Korean Cultural Heritage: Fine Arts*, Korea Foundation, 1994.

Various authors, *Fragrance of Korea: The Gilt-bronze Incense Burner of Baekje*, Korea Foundation, 2005.

Audio Visual Material

Korean Broadcasting System (KBS), "Nation of Gold & History of Gold", *History Special Documentary Series*, KBS Media, 2002.

Korean Broadcasting System (KBS), "Koryo Buddhist Paintings: The World of Super-Precision", *History Special Documentary Series*, KBS Media, 2006.

Korean Spirit and Culture Website

www.kscpp.net

All booklets published in the series are available on our website, as well as additional materials covering various aspects of Korean history and culture.

Published so far:

Admiral Yi Sun-sin

King Sejong the Great

Chung Hyo Ye

Fifty Wonders of Korea

Taste of Korea

Online video library includes:

Korean Cuisine

Hanbok, the Clothes of Nature

Traditional Dance and Music

A Sparking Journey to Korea

UNESCO World Heritage in Korea

And more…

Published by Korean Spirit & Culture Promotion Project

Korean Spirit & Culture Promotion Project is a 501(c)(3) not for profit organization that was formed under the Diamond Sutra Recitation Group (Chungwoo Buddhist Foundation) in October 2005 to promote Korean history and culture. KSCPP has been publishing and distributing free booklets and DVDs on Korean heritage. Please direct all inquries to kscpp@diamondsutra.org.

New York
158-16 46th Ave., Flushing, NY 11358
☎ 718 539-9108
New Jersey
190 Mountain Rd, Ringoes, NJ 08551
☎ 609-333-9422
Los Angeles
2197 Seaview Dr, Fullerton, CA 92833
☎ 562-644-8949
Atlanta
2100 Bishop Creek Drive, Marietta,
GA 30062 ☎ 770-640-1284

Korea
131-80 Seongbuk ? dong, Scongbuk-gu
Seoul 136-824
☎ 82-2-742-0172
Germany
Hiltistr, 7a 86916 Kaufering
☎ 49-8191-70618
England
57 Amberwood Rise, New Malden,
Surrey KT3 5JQ
☎ 44-208-942-1640

* When you finish this booklet, please donate it to a library or school so that it can be shared with others. It would also be greatly appreciated if you could leave your comments and impressions in the guestbook at www.kscpp.net or www.koreanhero.net. Thank you.

Front Gold crown made in Korea about 1500 years ago, worn by a queen. Of the ten gold crowns from ancient times extant in the world today, eight were made in Korea. This crown is considered to be the most exquisite and delicate of them all. Height 27.5cm, Silla Dynasty, 5-6th century AD, National Treasure No. 191, Seoul National Museum. **Rear** Gold earrings made in Korea about 1400 years ago. Each earring is decorated with 5000 gold granules of 0.7mm in diameter. Diameter 3.5cm, Length 8.3cm, Silla Dynasty, 6th century AD, National Treasure No. 90, Seoul National Museum.

ISBN 978-0-9797263-1-6